SCENES
FROM THE
CEREBELLUM

A Poetic Experience

STARK HUNTER

Scenes From the Cerebellum

A Poetic Experience by Stark Hunter

Published by Mind Tavern Books, 2019
Cover art by Stephanie M. Moore

…you have not seen these villages in your lifetime. They exist as clouds in a swift-moving memory; these clouds know the sounds of passion and longings…and heartbreak…

Poetry written 2018-19
by Stark Hunter

Copyright 2019 by Stark Hunter
All rights reserved

Paperback ISBN: 978-1-63337-293-1
LCCN: 2019908763

Table Of Contents

Introduction

Scenes from the Cerebellum is the 9th literary work to be released through Mind Tavern. It is easy to say that it is extremely difficult to describe exactly what this book is, was or will be. Maybe the best way to explain these pages is: It's a "ghost book," a book about death, the Ultimate Reality in life. The Big Jump. The one event in life we are all waiting for. Included therein is a veritable phalanx of mental and photographic images abounding and manifesting on the pages like hundreds of ectoplasmic filaments, squirming out of my mind in the form of poetic excursions for the curious reader to absorb. As with many poetic works, this one screams the same: This is personal! What poetry isn't? So don't take anything in this book personally. And, not that it means anything, this will be my last work to be published in print book form. Opus 9 sounds complete.

Along for the poetic ride in this volume is my life-long, fellow artist, friend and present-day poetic collaborator, D. Lee. I have collaborated with The Dude both poetically and musically since 1969. For this volume, we worked together on five poems presented in Part 4, all written at Lee's home in the eastern hills of Santa Maria, California during the years 2017-2019. The cover artwork was done by Stephanie Moore. All of the photographs in this volume are from the author's personal collection, and are hereby copyrighted.

Once again, my technical collaboration with Emily Hitchcock at Proving Press in the concrete creation of this book was very smooth and easy. Thank you.

So, let us begin with this poetic knock at the door...

Stark Hunter

July, 2019

I. Scenes From the Culmen

First Poem in a Year

Are we crazy, or what?

Are we so special that we think the whole universe revolves around us?

Are we so cocksure that all this killing in the streets

Is just a normal part of life and living?

I turn my head away. "I don't want to see it"

"Move your mind to the throbbing compass.

Move your heart to the backward-turning wheel.

Take four steps to the side.

Take three more steps to the rear!

And take three of these to offset the other two."

I take no responsibility!

I plead not guilty if it pleases the court!

I seek no regress of grievances!

Hey, I'm cool!

But the fools on the hills bark

Like sad hounds into a silent starless night.

They have had their tongues cut out!

The poets of the mountains have lost their bellowing voices!

The dead of a thousand graveyards have begun to awaken!

And the light of a million stars has begun to fade!

"The blackness has set in for this day, tomorrow and the next!"

My friends, now the skyhawks pitch their spreading wings in earnest!

My friends, they know the answers to a thousand unasked questions.

"Are you saying something to me?"

"Are you saying nothing to me?"

 "Say nothing. Don't say something."

"Say nothing as you say something."

"What are you saying?"

"I don't know what I'm saying because

I'm lost in this crazy world,

This bumbling drunken beast of injustice and…"

"Are you saying something to me?"

Four Short Poems for the Apocalypse

Poem #1 – "Reality Bites"

Feeling so hopeless.

Feeling the loss somewhere inside.

I can feel it, but I don't know quite where.

Reality bites.

Feeling so awkward and sad.

I knew it was bound to happen.

But still,

I can't get it out of my mind.

The last time I saw her,

There in that stuffy smelly room,

She was shooing the demons away.

It is true.

The gods make those who are about to die

As mad as gadflies

Without blood to suck.

Reality bites.

Feeling so empty.

Feeling the loss somewhere inside.

I thanked the stars the night she died.

Poem #2 – "Part Biscuit Part Bone"

I shiver when I think about it.

Getting' up at four in the morning to walk six miles.

There is only one fool who would do such a thing.

My brain is sometimes cracked like my sidewalk.

It must be part biscuit, part bone.

But when I walk in the darkness

The entire world is mine.

I am the only one alive

And I salute the ghosts in the shadows.

They want my soul

And I want their ethereal essences.

I shiver when I think about it.

Maybe death is like a walk at four.

There is only one fool who would think that.

It must be part biscuit, part bone.

Poem #3 – "Baked Babylon"

Squeezing the forceps, handlessly

Like a pair of tweezers with no grip.

I groan and suffer alone.

Like Grover Cleveland back in 1892

When his cancerous jaw was dug into

By mustached doctors wearing pink carnations,

Digging and gouging and tugging

Like some gravedigger looking for soft earth.

Baked Babylon is my grease.

Let it smoke and oilize.

I want death for myself, no one else.

One billion children do not deserve the incineration.

Poem #4 – "Why Am I Thinking?"

Why am I thinking?

Is it because I stink?

Is it because I'm stuck breathing?

Why am I dying?

Is it because life is a game with no winners?

Is it because I seek pleasure in a world of pain?

Why am I crying?

is it because life is so futile?

Is it because death is the best part?

Why am I thinking?

Is it because I can't help it?

Can't help stopping the inevitable?

Oh death!

You wait for me over there,

Like a forlorn lover,

Behind shaded curtains in the night.

From the Nostril Vortex

I breathe in your perfumed

Plasma leaves from the nostril vortex.

I thrive in the pleasant scenes and velvet touchings.

I wince like a skybird earthbound.

Dare to escape from me.

Dare to hide in the dark.

Shhhh! Don't make a sound.

I am dancing without shoes in the moonlight.

I am waltzing with precise pre-planned movements in space.

I am spewing out movements that show you and me,

The two of us, walking the precise path to here and there,

And then finally to the place of all endings,

And like the cool morning mist, death enters unseen.

"It's the tomb! I'm in the tomb!

Mother, Father come get me here in the dark!"

But first, slowly slowly slowly…

I lift up her leg there in the shadows,

And I caress, and smell and lick.

"I have found the best time!

This is the most excellent moment!"

I was there in the dusty places,

I was hanging nearby with all of you.

I was wet with unimagined enticings,

Weary, oh so world-weary to the nucleus of my bones!

Of tentatively living all the years of a dubious lifetime,

And of finally dying in the dry ditches of twenty thousand days.

"Come here honey, kiss me now, here in the distant cemetery.

We can hold on to each other

As the mad earth spins into oblivion.

"Sir, would you be so kind?

Some mindful enterprise and

The Pretext Syllogism combo.

And I will have a side of nomenclature

And for dessert two heapings of existential mind mysogenation,

Topped with granulated mesomorphic nom de plume!

Dancing, dancing, dancing and holding on.

She and me sweating in the black heat.

No other way to live.

No other way to breathe.

"I am just here.

See? Know what I mean?

I was born into this like all of you!

I had nothing to say about it.

What do ya say, honey? What do ya say?"

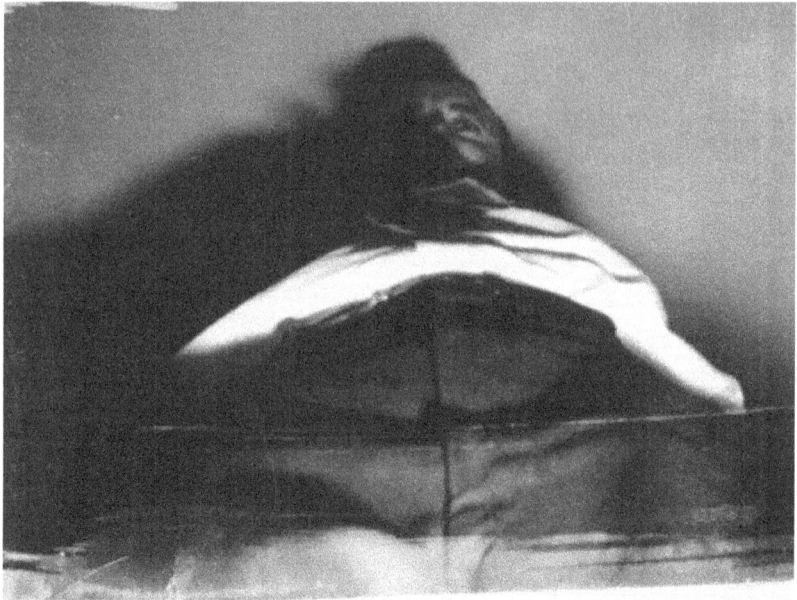

"...there is no death...here, take this turtle oil and rub it in deeply... there is no turning from the shadow...painted nails with Mexican silences...eyes alighted in the darkness...we will speak the truthful moments as they come to us...we will accept that which we must accept...in days of windy confusions, and nights of still determinations...still, I wonder what you are thinking as you rub that oil over your brown skin, as you sit there with bare legs crossed, leaning in close, like an old lover from another planet in time...i can see you are lonely, and in need of the human touch, and I want to take you to the garden, my garden, where the lemon trees mate with the dead men's bones."

There is Nothing to Say About It

There is nothing to say about it

No words to describe it at all

There are no words at all to describe

the mass slaughter of innocents,

the relentless malignant progressions of

the evil black-moving cloud of terminations,

the toxic metastasizing ooze of outright annihilations,

the blood-gurgling regurgitations, and

the blood-spurting decapitations.

There is nothing to say about it.

Nothing to say at all.

No words to describe

the hopeless piercing cries of the infidels

the whimpering terrified pleadings of the condemned

the silent gasping inhalations of the dying

There is nothing to say about it.

No words to describe it at all!

My heart at 62 years has not seen anything like this at all!

Never anything like this at all!

I have not seen this outrageous slaughter before at all!

There is nothing to say, except...

These are the days!

The days of this unkind hour;

the days before the great onslaught!

Before this massive earthly descent to the lowest places,

the smelly dank places,

the rotting miasma of the dead places.

There are no words to describe it!

There is nothing to say at all!

We Are The Watchers

Into the breach the multitudes surge,

Into the crushing breakers and

Beyond the sucking mindless tides,

Down down into the whirring, rushing confluence,

Precipitously we fall and slide,

Tenuously and tragically we slip.

We are the watchers of the wasted!

We are the watchers of the dancing dead!

We have seen them bring in the living.

We have silently closed our eyes to their madness.

We are the watchers of the delirious and of the distressed.

Falling, falling trying to seize a toehold,

Trying to stop desperately this inevitable plunge,

This meshing melting plummet,

This fatal succumbing to hate and ignorance,

This downward drowning into the watery abyss of anarchy,

This insane enveloping

This resounding de-evolution into one massive heartbreak.

We are the human machine!

That lurches and stalls in the swell,

Spewing bloody angst

And the sooty smoke of smothering fear.

We are the star climbers!

The mountain gazers!

We are the watchers of the wasted.

We are the watchers of the diseased.

We have seen them bring in the living

We have seen the fires of Armageddon!

Burning burning furiously in the firmament,

And we have heard the crescendoing cries of the forgotten.

We are the watchers of the wasted!

We are the watchers of the dancing dead!

Word Quintet in C Major

Open the door my friend,

Climb on in,

Join me here in this relentless caravan,

This unstoppable, this incontrovertible,

this inexorable movement,

To the depths of the dry gulf.

Join me here my friend,

In this annihilating armada,

This incontrovertible migration,

This inexorable swarm

To the watery crossroads of the dry places,

To the liquid asphalt of insipid time!

I stare at you from across the room here.

I stare and gawk and hawk at you,

And I feel the pelting rain of desire.

You look good over there, sitting

With beautiful gleaming crossed legs.

"Sorry, beg your pardon,

I say, but have we not met before?

Did we not share beers on the Terrace of Tyre

At sunset?

Did we not tell each other stories,

Old stories of love and betrayal and heartbreak?

At sunset?

Did we not look away from each other,

When stories of new love suddenly emerged,

As with a new sunrise?"

My friend, there is no

Escape from this throbbing hole, no

Escape from this cold numbing wind,

This whirlingly insane wind

Of cold blasts of killing ice.

And I ride here

Ride like a sweating Sultan,

Astride the mighty beast of Tyre!

Perched high in rich raiment,

I wave to the multitudes

I send a salute to the throng!

I ride shotgun here

Ride nice and easy

Like a tanning garçon on his off day,

Like a sitting trog waiting wistfully,

Waiting waiting for gams not intended for him.

My friend, the world turns and turns,

It turns today and tomorrow,

It will turn as the river turns in spring,

It will turn as a woman's heart turns,

When eyes that once stared ahead, now look away.

It will turn my friends because it has to!

Riding, Riding, Riding....

Downhill now! The insane wind

Assaults me. Harasses me. Accosts me.

It presses its loose lips upon my face,

It seeks the mad blood of passion!

"Let us calm ourselves

Reassure ourselves

That all is right and as planned.

Let us all look at one another!

Let us all nod in agreement!

The days ahead will manifest themselves,

Transfigure themselves,

As blooms upon the water lilies.

...that orange sky at sunset...that compelling October
twilight, as something unseen and unheard led the boy to
the shore...kneeling on two of those smooth river rocks,
he craned his neck upward and saw the silvery thing...
high above the rapids of the Sacramento...

Heliotrome

A fly with green translucent scales

Is bothering me to the brink of insanity!

This irksome beast buzzes around my ears,

My mouth and my nose, and I know,

As I know this old quiver of mine,

That this beast must die!

What haven't the authorities swatted it down prior to today?

Do I not pay some form of tax to rid these abominations from my life?

"Hello Honey. Would you care for some veal?

I like your pearl necklace there. ..

it reminds me of an afternoon at your house…"

"And what afternoon was that Gilbert?"

"Oh I'm sure you remember Mercedes. Think about it.

I still have your… garment, in my desk drawer."

"Not at all Gilbert, I am sure. But I will have the veal."

The flies!

There are millions of flies dominating my house!

Please do you have any suggestions, any advice,

As to what I should do about these pests?

She enters. She is naked.

Her figure is of a greek goddess.

Her breasts are firm and full, and her nipples

Are hardened as she speaks… shhh.

"There was once a beautiful woman who sat in a tree.

She always watched when the day began

And when the day ended.

When the sun rose, she cried, and when it set, she laughed.

She had a dog named Catharsis.

At night the dog slept in the garden by the tree,

Amidst the "dead man's fingers" there.

The woman hooted like an owl as she sat there

In that tree, and ate raspberries.

She was never seen by anyone, except me.

She told me, actually told me I had deep eyes.

She said my soul was like a river, a deep,

Swiftly-flowing river with a tower there,

A little ways down, on the muddy bank.

And up on top of the tower, there are little boys

Spitting into the river below."

"Enjoying the view.

I enjoy it indeed when a beautiful woman wears a short skirt

And artfully shows off her appendages.

But Mercedes, please, it pains me too much

To see your amazingly sexy legs over there,

And not be able to do anything about it!

Please spare me!"

"Naughty boy! Then stop looking at them.

Besides, I have nothing to hide from you."

"Evidently not, Miss."

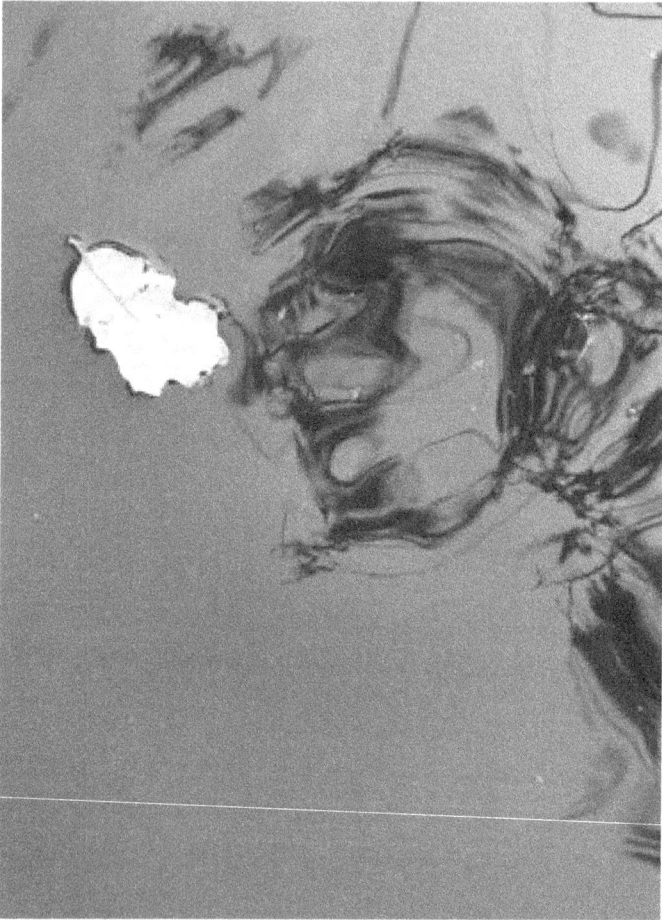

"...future time comes at us, like crazy light rays penetrating through the open boards at sunrise, coming at you like a flying tray, with sweet and sour sauces for the dipping… except sometimes, when the moon above slips behind a dark vaporous cloud, I wonder if it is too late… too late to drink from this empty cup…here take my hand… we can create a new future, sans the thrown rocks, and the dead leaves…come here…let's sit close together, and celebrate the ceremonies of young desire…turn out the lights…whisper…they don't think we're here…"

The Silvery Scenes

The silvery scenes,

Above the sensuous Mexican bloom,

Of transcendent yellow, red and orange,

Back there – in the digesting side garden,

Next door, adjacent the obscene lemon flowers,

An old sot sits and peruses

A darkened shuttered window upstairs.

Blue sky and creeping streaks of contumacious white,

Soar as sky ghosts,

A pitch above the silent stares,

And the forgotten entreaties;

The old sot remembers a long-ago morning in May,

Thirty years hence, years indeed

Filled with wandering gazes and

Imagined gaspings at day's end.

You, the young girl of Mexican skin,

With eyes of the earth,

18 years old, and at last ready,

Ready for the great cosmic conquest,

You, spying and staring at the man,

Up there on the hill.

Using strong legs and decisive fingers,

I tended my garden, seemingly oblivious,

To your silent inert gazing,

Your self-embraces of squealing frustration,

There in your secret steamy spot,

Behind the darkened unshuttered window upstairs,

Translucent as a dragonfly,

You, thinking forbidden thoughts,

Of wild silvery scenes in the secret shadows,

With the man tending his garden,

And though alone and detached,

You, the young mexican girl next door,

Hiding behind that unshuttered window upstairs,

Knew nothing of his wild designs,

Nothing of his intended episodes,

The silvery scenes in the secret shadows,

Back there- above the sensuous Mexican bloom.

Word Requiem in E Minor

Hey my friend,

Look over there, yonder through the myrtles,

Can you see them? The living dead,

Burying the dirt of a million graves,

Embalming the streets with their dead screams.

Oh please, grace us with a few words.

No one in our family ever got buried,

Without a scripture reading or a baptizing.

Silently they pass by the deceased one,

These undead dead.

Everyday I hear them moan and wail,

Everyday I see them saunter like doomed peacocks;

These undead dead.

"Welcome friends to this slaughter of evil.

Please join me as we pray to the Unseen;

Perhaps a cool cocktail for your cold mechanized souls?

Oh, I do find you creatures so low and so needy, indeed!

You are just statues.

Just soulless heartless statues, that move,

Screaming statues that squirm and writh,

Like mindless snakes in a furnace.

Look at me, my friends!

You are not alive!

Though you move and process thought,

You do not exist!

Though you inhale and exhale,

There is no life in you.

There is no sequence or spasm within you.

I now pronounce all of you dead!"

Hey my friend,

Look over there, yonder through the mytles,

Can you see them? The living dead,

Burying the dirt of a million graves,

Embalming the streets with their dead screams.

Word Trio in D Minor

Who? Me?

Dude, I'm just a confused star-watcher like you.

The movie of life continually plays before us,

Here in the cinematic darkness of another dying day;

Celluloid memories dressed in black parade before us like lost ghosts;

We sad souls, hopeful but hopeless,

Scan the heavens for a distant voice, a silent nod,

Even for a faint whisper of response,

From the Giver and Taker of all.

For the Bitch, dressed scantily in baleful blue,

Continues to turn and bend like Eden's snake;

Moist, slippery oozing scenes take place once again in the leafy
    palisades.

We star-watchers know where to gaze,

We choose which stars to kill with an empty barrel.

The asphalt avenues remind us of the nights ahead,

They veer as a woman veers,

After bitter recognitions in the morning,

After anguished eyes have seen the drooling truth;

They confront us as dust confronts the dead,

They guide us as lanterns in the cold fog.

They know the truth is hidden in plain sight.

Who? Me?

Dude, I'm just another lost soul like you.

Lost as men without contemplation or reconciliation;

Lost as women without gesture or spasm, but

We star-watchers will bring roses for the dead,

We will sing the songs of submission and survival;

We will dance to the music of madness,

And we will continue to scan the skies and the stars

For a distant voice, a silent nod,

Even for a faint whisper of response,

From the Giver and Taker of all.

Though Unseen

Racism oozes inside there, though unseen,

Just vibrating there with incredible fangs for punctures;

Far inside the nucleus of our frenzied souls,

It throbs knowingly there, like a silent spider,

Deep inside the focal core of sentient breathing.

It cannot be educated away into obsolescence.

It cannot be legislated into social edicts for the fools.

Alas, it is fear that directs the spasms of hate.

It is the suave cocktail for the blind ones, the dying ones;

They play the games of the spiritually comatose.

"Shhh, find the light switch lady in white…shhh…"

It is behind the crusted door beneath the eaves;

It is oozing there, though unseen.

Just vibrating there, fangs ready for the sucking.

Find it fast inside there,

In the dim corner of last year's cobwebs,

Amongst the eaten sweaters and forgotten umbrellas.

"Shhh, find the light switch lady in black… shhh…"

It is the only solution to the hate thing…

Find it fast, and sip the sweet nectar of healing.

Of Fond Amusements

The soaring sinews of morning sunrise,

Ascend like attacking phantoms with flailing spears;

They rise thinking of fond amusements in the foggy darkness;

They appear as an apparition appears through an old curtain,

As a suffering ghost lurking, groaning in the back room there,

In the old back mansion

Amidst the dark tuft of beckoning willows,

Out back, hidden and forbidden, their erotic shadows.

Then we stand close together,

I have my fingers on Cape Hatterus,

Gently and firmly, as ripe apples in the wind

Topple, I guided you breathlessly amongst the doilies.

I let my masticating mind fixate visions of contorting sweat.

I, as a force of destiny,

Spiraled straight into boneless sockets.

Don't move female person, you, with wafts of perfume strong,

Stare into me female person, stare into my eyes,

There is no other river to cross,

The boa constrictors have put on blinders.

They don't see you. They don't care.

But I do. As a lone bloom on a strong myrtle branch,

I see you over there,

As much as the sky sees our rising voices,

But now my brain hears your voice,

Yet you are silent.

Word Sonata in B Flat (in 5 Movements)

You know exactly what you're doing.

You sit in that short red skirt, and

Cross your shiny tan legs, there. Now you

Lean over with full cleavage exposed,

And partake in another draw of smoky seduction;

You can see the dollar signs in my knowing eyes,

And I can see lovely times at poolside,

In your short skirt, and dark glasses.

So cheers! To us, just a couple of cool cats,

Two old hippies,

With lemon drinks, glass bongs, and feathered toys,

Conversing wordlessly in eye language,

Under the searing unzipping sun,

Embracing the approaching nakedness.

Laying out in a chaise lounge with white noses,

Just drying out our souls and bodies,

Drying out our differences with the holding of a draw.

Pass it over here sweetie.

I feel it too, as you sit there,

Staring at me like I'm the package you were expecting,

Last week when the mails didn't come through,

Due to the storm, and the mud and the misery.

I enjoy women like you.

As you sit there in your short red skirt.

There is a mysterious gloss covering everything you say,

A gooey gloss that smells of electrical wiring,

Something that might make a person sick,

Or maybe bring back a stubborn memory you forgot about

For decades, because you were lost,

Lost inside a rolled-up carpet,

An old rain-ruined rug from 1958, or so,

When times in the backseat meant something to a person.

Now look at us, just a couple of cool cats,

Two old hippies,

Bored and resigned,

Passing reefer until the stoned moment is realized.

Yes, just sitting here looking at you,

I can tell,

You know exactly what you're doing.

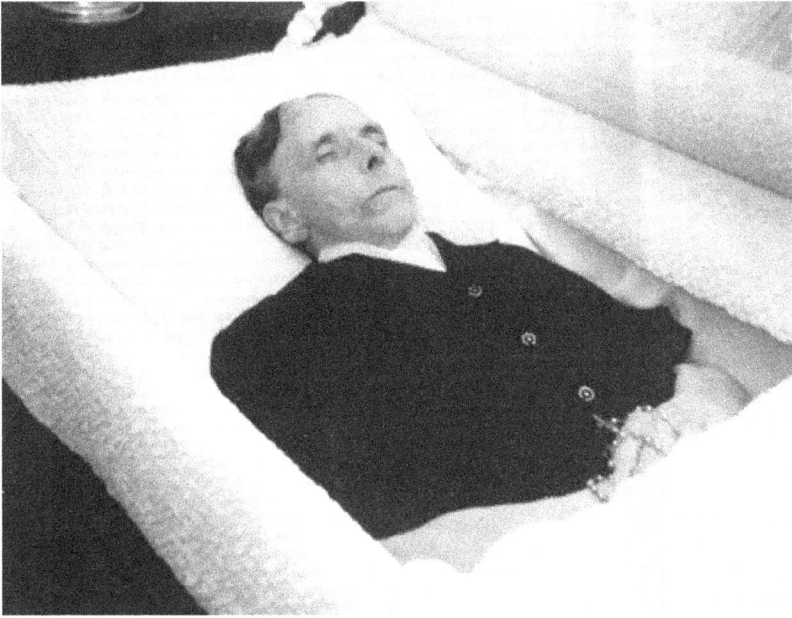

"...step inside here, but be ever careful with the furniture… I wonder if she will open her eyes…any second now she may sit up in that beige box and say how it was all just a lark, just to fool everyone because, well, what else can one do, when life has come to an end, of sorts…kindly blow out the candle, the flowers here are wilting and dying, and she might start to turn…the big turning is transpiring…hear it? The big turning.…"

"...Inside this box we have soiled socks and dry biscuits for the dog... and hidden underneath the floor are the gold pieces, and the bones from a hundred forgotten days...and on top of that shelf are the remains of a universe of dust mites, most of which have met their own relative armageddon, eons of time ago...and beside the lamp stand stands my friend, hello friend. let us exit this door onto the porch, enclosed with bricks and cement... and there is the shadow...turning as it must..."

Word Rhapsody in C Sharp Minor

Existent.

The new emitting emotion, a flat one.

It is the deepest of lost human thoughts;

It takes you nowhere beyond any unseen border;

It leaves you in a gray cloud of indistinction;

It peels the flatness of drudgery in unkind ways;

There is no wisdom in flatness,

No inner satisfaction in all that breathes there;

Like a flattened gnawing of foolish striving,

The feeling that all is parallel with itself abides. Indeed,

We are meant to swim and soar as rays at feeding time.

You look at me like an eel from its dark hole,

Fathoms below the surface of sinister tides.

You unbutton your lust with descending eyes.

"Miss, kindly unbutton the next, and

As a tandem in eternity,

We shall establish new truths for the fools!"

Striding the dark voluminous hallway, you and I,

Amidst these wide-eyed walls,

Alive with crawling wallpaper,

Of dismal serpentine scenes in the theater,

We kissed passionately in the faraway corner, there,

Under the blinking chandelier, as it tinkles,

Where this grand hall leads is my dream immemorial,

It leads to you, just you of the billions deserted here.

"Take my hand and allow the movements

Of my carnivorous music to overtake you,

To overwhelm you with my carousing arousals,

Sustained with the slithering crescendos of eel music."

I can hear it cascading through the opaque windows,

Of you and me in the shadowy distances,

Touching sweaty finger tips in the dark,

Rubbing expectantly, licking lasciviously,

As with all stones in the tumult of time;

We the tandem weavers

Pick our pears for the slicing.

Singular and Angular

I could play the piano

In such a charming enchanting way,

A way that could render the girl

With the dark eyes completely

At my expressed command,

Into a braid of mystical tension, such as it is,

Tension for men who understand

Long lustful looks in old hallways,

Sitting in old armchairs with pleated patterns,

Only the hobknobbers seem to understand these crazed adventures,

With dimmed lamps and zippers released,

She has been with the curious boys,

The biting insatiable boys in their locked towers.

I have seen the bronze statues of living goddesses there,

Naked and pointed,

Perfumed-sweetened bodies,

Twisting and spasming,

With silks and satins

Laying haphazardly

Behind candle-lit curtains,

And the boys pouncing

Upon open encroachments.

"**... go up this street,** and turn left…at the stop, turn right… go west on Beverly…cross the railroad tracks and then the river… turn right at the first signal…go north on the parkway for about a mile…turn right at Abbeywood…go around the corner…turn left at Noyes…go about 200 yards…you'll see a green house on the left… park in the driveway…under the green awning…I will see you then…goodbye…"

Talk of the Table

(June, 1968)

"Baby, there is this lustful mischief in your eyes,

And this compelling sky-tense color,

Staring at me like azure apples,

Shimmering inert on the kitchen table,

Ready for the carving."

"Sweet honey, know that I worship your lips;

They remind me of…

Fresh strawberries oozing mindlessly in whipped cream."

"Come here baby, I want to kiss you now…

I want to drag you down here,

And eat your daily bread,

Then drink your nightly white wine,

With one swallow."

"Mm, nice. I love the taste of your monster,

Give me its heart…

Ahhh, more kisses, mmm…

Wet pursed kisses,

That make me forget about tomorrow."

"Here, in the steamy shadows,

I crave your animal movements,

Your firm persuasive grip."

"Go slow baby, ahh, go ever so slowly, always slowly…

Here in this lush perfume garden, ooh...

This ripe pulsating garden of...screaming flowers!"

"Sweet honey...please,

My breathing needs your breathing,

And my lips plead for your erect impulses!"

"Ahh, oooh... no words can describe this...

No words, but

I am undead!"

(June, 1969)

"I can see death in your itchy eyes, baby,

You wish to kill me.

I know it from watching your trembling hands,

As you stand there gawking,

Dangling that big dagger,

Like some deviant butcher,

Drooling before the slaughter,

Ready for the carving."

"And no finer pig than thee, honey,

Tied and trussed there, with no one to help you!"

"Please baby, you can't be serious, please,

I do not wish to die!"

"Shhh... my sweet honey.

Death is just a relative matter.

Shhh....now, now, don't cry.

Sooner or later, we all must enter into the unkind hour;

We must all be brave."

"Stop baby! Stop! The pain is too much!

Arrrrgh! Please!"

"Sweet honey, be still, for this sinister comedy has just begun!

Ha ha ha ha! And now,

I will slice off the other ear for my salad tonight! Ha ha ha!"

"Arrrrrrgh! Please baby! Stop!

Stop this pain, and all this blood which spills from me!"

"Ah yes my sweet, yes,

But I do enjoy the gesticulations of a sloth!

Slowly, slowly I shall proceed,

One finger at a time,

One toe after the next,

Offering absolutions in my black vestments here,

I, the high priest of your trembling funeral!

I shall serve your screams to the repenters!

I will bless the throng with a final cut!"

"Arrrgh..., no... words can describe this...

No words, but

I am dead!"

Fulcrum

Listen to me sweetheart.

It is easy to be a fool.

It requires no intelligence at all.

You will always listen to those who speak

Words you personally want to hear.

You will always ignore and belittle those

Who disagree with your tentative notion

Of what the definitive truth is.

If you say the earth is round,

And there is a tone of finality in your voice,

I will say, fine, but I disagree.

I say it is flat, and I'm right because, well,

I have more college degrees than you,

I am obviously smarter than you,

I'm whiter than you,

And have more money than you.

My house is bigger than yours,

And my car is faster.

Besides, flat objects don't turn

Elliptically in circles that

Continue on and on, ad infinitum,

Without some kind of radical transmogrification

Occurring in its plain and acute geometric form.

What would Einstein say?

He would agree with me of course!

He would say: "Two things are infinite,

The Universe, and human stupidity."

Here sweetheart, have another chaser.

I detest talking politics with you,

But I love talking about Einstein,

And I love watching you sit there,

Showing off your shiny scented legs,

As you cross and uncross them

Restlessly.

Here, give me your foot,

I will massage your toes with cotton swabs,

And peanut butter,

And I will feed you my electric eel eggs.

The Next Hitler

The next Hitler will execute the world's masses,

Using costly powerful pharmaceuticals;

Feel-good grenades that bring euphoric explosions.

Metal bombs and bullets belong to a former age,

An old-school time when murder was expensive.

Whereas confining thousands of prisoners in camps,

Well, that is certainly not cost-effective either.

Food to feed these worthless ones

Requires a fortune in gold.

Best to leave the stressed masses alone,

Let them work for pitiful wages.

Let them toil and suffer as animals in barren times.

We will sit back and watch, and wait,

As they slide into addiction's vagina,

Unable to think, move or breathe.

"**shh...**don't make a sound...it's my father going into the kitchen...shh...no, he didn't see you...it's too dark in here,,," green carpet and wooden destinies...she drove the Camaro down to Hadley, and turned right..." Was there ever a time when we did not sneak off to some corner in the darkness?..."

Detritus

Sitting there, honey,

Cleansed and bathed,

Scented with lilac and rose,

Glistening at your dressing table, and

Eyeing yourself in the chrome mirror;

I, as your guest, sit by and watch,

Astonished at your well-intentioned revealings,

Seeing your young beauty at morning tide,

As hands and fingers apply the detritus,

To nineteen year-old eyes,

Awash in teen wisdom.

I sense there is something you want to say,

As you lean toward your reflection there,

Smearing scarlet on wet open lips,

Your unbuttoned camisole dangling loosely,

Upon your shimmering backside,

But finding a foothold upon your upturned breast.

And here I sit, astonished again,

At the perennial return of one endless ritual

After another.

Zounds!

Do you realize I cannot resist you?

Yet it makes me wonder,

If you want me to make love to you.

Yes, I wonder.

Well, shall we just dispense

With this slow dance in the darkness?

Look at me!

Zounds!

I will make you dance!

Cathexis

I see you silhouetted in a vague haze,

On the far end of this breathing hallway,

Way off in the strange distance there,

Amid the suffocating cigarette smoke,

And the obscene wallpaintings,

Of nude pale women wearing necklaces,

Reposed motionless on verandas by the Seine.

Then, I look and see you squatting there,

Under the tinkling chandeliers,

Aglow as with a halo,

Sainted only when wearing white lace,

As you are now, goddess of mine!

Shhh! Listen!

I hear violins outside, two or three of them,

Playing Traumerie in the rain.

Come here, and let us explore with blindfolds,

This side room of esoteric pleasures.

Shhh…It is unlocked, and there are pillows inside,

Numerous soft cotton pillows,

Piled wall to wall, up to the knees,

And the elbows.

Come here, goddess of mine,

And let us dive into this tundra

Of plush velvety incinerations,

This mind field of amazing meltings.

Symbiosis

Sitting on that rock

Like a suburban mermaid,

You look like a lost girl

With a long sad story to tell.

So honey, why don't we

Mosey on over to Wide-track Town,

Where the freeways meet in purgatory;

There are singing hipsters there,

Dressed in the regalia of the deranged,

Sniffing salt through straws,

There are ten thousand latex surfers

Returning from the dead,

Returning from their brief sojourn

In the distant backwaters,

The yellowish green sulfur waters,

That seep into your bare flesh,

And send mad biting impulses

Straight into your seething soul.

Ah, yes! So, how long have you had that…

Pardon me honey, but,

Is that a bruise on your neck?

Or maybe it is the love-bite I recently

Gave you, as we rode in the back seat

Of a lavender blue 72' Land Yacht,

Spread out fine under a blanket,

As Broten, up front, steered us down the long highway,

Through a lit-up suburbia,

Like a chrome dragon spitting smoke from its butt.

Kissing you, honey, is a meal unto itself.

Like eating electric spit

With a dash of salt!

Now is the time,

Now is the moment to touch you.

If you don't want me to,

I won't…

Sitting on that rock,

Just like a seducing mermaid.

So, honey, what exactly is your story?

Why don't we mosey on over to Wide-track Town?

We can talk incessantly until the stars appear,

We can watch the latex surfers find nirvana,

And I can give your daring thigh,

My thirty-minute love bite.

"who are these ghosts working here, amongst the orange shadows, and the fence slats, alive again from 1935... 'what would I do without me pipe and me beer...'

Antithesis

In May, the lion's ear blooms immaculately,

As if the night sky is on fire.

It excretes a ravishing untarnished beauty,

A mesmerizing compelling beauty

Only the mad mystics and poets can discern.

Here, put on these rubber sandals;

The pair with the ostrich plumes,

For the walkway to my hidden tower is replete,

With thorns, bristles and stickers; the ladder there

Has splinters that anesthetize one's toes,

Your plump white toes with the crimson polish,

Applied there like bloody footsteps on murderous floors.

There is nothing we can do to offset the numbing,

Except, pretend we never met or kissed that time,

When we decided to dare the gods of crescendoing passion.

I remember you decided unilaterally

To disrobe inside my '72 Land Yacht,

For fear of eternally disappointing me.

"Here, take my hat and cover yourself."

Indeed, you are the antithesis of me.

But now, let us walk to my high garlanded tower,

A mile and a quarter from here,

Where we will sit naked on velvet carpet,

And rub thumbs in the candle light,

As Debussy music inundates our sated senses,

From speakers attached to the walls like bison heads,

Surrounded by insect-slaughtered window panes,

And glass bongs that spew atoms of electric sex.

Relax honey, it's wonderful you're so open-minded.

Relax, you will love the interesting insides

Of my tall and comfortable tower, where

We will observe the unfolding continuing tragedies,

Of dire human existence; it will be

Just like reading old newspapers from 1968, black print

Still greasy with unslaughtered fish, complete

With disastrous headlines no one wants to remember. But

We, you and I, will remember them, and weep a little,

When the mad dancing inevitably commences,

Here, inside and beside our grinding bodies.

Look over there, honey.

Do you see the lion's ear blooming immaculately?

Do you hear their soft cries whimpering in the night,

Like virgin lovers squealing in the darkness?

Yes honey, we can hear their invisible sighs and moans,

From the top of my high

And comfortable tower.

Gallimaufry

Your sandals make a strange mixing sound,

As we step together down this shadowy path,

Past the innumerable tufts of Sprygen weed,

Where old farmers once hoofed to the music

Of the Elkhorns, and the Spitters.

We will soon eat from their generous platters,

Abandoned in the ice houses south of Belchork.

Piled high with sugared meats and bitter olives.

We will sit in plush lacquered chairs there,

Chairs of sandlewood, and mystic topaz.

We will be staring into each other's eyes,

Globular orbs of azure fascinations,

Seeking unspoken permission to stare yet more,

But as an encore, at a pair of different eyes.

We will embrace behind sheer curtains of lapis lazuli,

Inside the vestibule with lotioned legs dangling.

We will move in infinite slowness,

We will seek the absolute devotions,

Of the shadow dances there.

We will listen to the singing sirenic voices

Of the Elkhorns and the Spitters,

Beckoning us with their spiral gyrations,

As sparkling mineral water is shared in goblets,

Encrusted with peridot and citrin.

We will at last find profound discovery,

Concealed within their mad enticings.

Proceed quietly, shh! Your sandals are noisy,

As we step together down this shadowy path,

Past the ice houses at Belchork,

Our lives and our consenting atoms

Enmeshed and entwined forever, with

The innumerable tufts of Sprygen weed.

Word Maneuvers in F Sharp Minor

As it goes, so it goes.

Imperceptibly.

As the languorous lizard soaks in the sun,

It's fat green belly filled with flies,

You and I will do the same, indeed,

We will find utter solace under a moving cloud,

We will wish for an escape from the piercing onslaught,

We will wish for an end to the pain and abject sadness,

Of daily life on this staggering planet;

But instead, as carnivorous time eats its way forward,

We too will be absorbed into the Beast,

Into which all are eventually swallowed whole,

We will be digested by the darkness.

As it goes, so it goes,

Imperceptibly.

As the languorous lizard soaks in the sun,

You and I will do the same.

We will spend our lives hunting,

And being hunted,

By the masticating microbes of infinite space;

We will all be an ingredient, at last,

In something else's soup.

And what is our end, honey?

What factors are there in our ultimate demise?

Here, give me your hand and let me hold it.

We will soon enter into the room of pillows.

It's down the dark meandering hallway,

Past the statue of a kneeling Artemis,

Inside, you will find fiery explosions;

That of instant death upon the battlements.

We will be vacant from the universe,

For a second....

As the blooming Centrix flower bends,

And waits for pulsing Time to ejaculate,

We will watch its wondrous presentations,

We will lie askew, and count our moles

With trembling erect appendages.

As it goes, so it goes,

Imperceptibly.

...and so it goes, at sunset, we stardust catchers must bring out the umbrella, lest the ions and photons of extreme exposures, would most imperceptibly sap us of what is necessary, in today's tedious timeline, of cheeseburgers with fries, diet soda with no ice, and tickets to another diversion under the lights, somewhere between here, and the last stop sign at the edge of town....the shadow with umbrella on the old wall, 1972...

II. Scenes From the Vermis

Precursives In A Minor

My dear, you are dead now, and

It follows that the dead cannot speak,

But please dear woman,

Utter however softly,

Your ghostly peep,

For we are your survivors,

Following soon,

As the buoy bell continues to toll,

Way out there in the dark bay.

My dearest one, you,

Now sunken and cold,

In your pearl-inlaid casket,

Your cozy bed of now,

Have found your final pillow.

Well I remember another pillow,

The one I gently rested your head upon,

That damp effusive evening,

When we, unfurled and tussling,

Inside our shadowy room of pillows,

Found a new kind of death.

You said 'Darling, light my cigarette,'

And I, with cuff links blazing,

Stroked your polished fingers with desire,

And said 'Of course dear,'

And then you covered yourself

With my rusty chapeau.

'Is that the buoy bell tolling again?

I can hear it through your breathing, and

Your relentless penetrations.'

No, there is nothing there, except

My dangling tongue,

Reaching in like a bear for the throat.

And yet, my dear,

You never turn away,

You always keep your long silent gaze,

When this dripping candle here,

Slowly fades, as it must.

Word Calibration in G Major

'Don't worry honey.

No one walks this way.

At least, not at this hour.'

The neons inside the dark house,

Across the street over there,

Are aglow with ghostly shadows,

Flickering like strobes in slow motion.

Just our car parked here now, and

No one is around. Nothing

Except Dream faeries dressed as opossums.

We are alone at last, and

It is time to touch firm bodies together.

It is time to be alive once again.

Your top two buttons are unfastened, I see.

Shh, be still as I unbutton the bottom two;

My left hand knows where to go;

I will now kiss and caress your soft perfumed neck,

As my searching fingers follow their bead.

'Shh, what's that sound?'

Loud voices coming this way,

Formless voices strolling by on parade;

'Shh, duck down and don't make a sound,'

As we continue to kiss and lick excited flesh,

Embracing in silent sweat,

Ensconced under a flaming white blanket,

Inside a lavender blue '72 Land Yacht.

There is a moonless sky outside, and

A creeping fog beginning to settle in.

'Ahh, I see that you are cold, honey.

Here is my hat,

Cover yourself.'

Word Lyric for Music #1
"Eating Religion at Midnight"

Saw Big Edith at the laundry mat,

Says she's got a bad case of stage fright,

But she's big and bad by all accounts,

Saw her eating religion at midnight.

Now Big Edith, she spit on the ground,

Pissed off she can't sing no more,

And now she sleeps alone under the moonlight,

Ain't no way she's anybody's whore,

Saw her eating religion at midnight.

Look at Big Edith, she dancing like a star,

She's finding karma with taps and strings,

She's finding love in the backseat of a blue car.

She's shuffling cards backwards in the candlelight

Saw her eating religion at midnight.

Big Edith, she flirts again at the brake house,

She's flashing rings for the cheating men,

She's told her sob story with fake tears,

Now Big Edith is dancing again.

She's finding salvation with a cross and a spear,

She's big and bad, and quite erudite,

Saw her eating religion at midnight.

Word Lyric for Music #2
"Sleeping In The Inkwell"

Been looking around for that strange smell,

Don't know if it's coming from under the sink.

I been sleeping in the inkwell,

I can only wonder what you must think.

I hear there's been a lot of loose talk,

Some dude talking smack about my babe,

But I been sleeping in the inkwell,

I wanted no part of that charade.

My babe, she left me,

High and dry in the summer,

She say I'm a liar, written in a note from her,

But I disagree.

She never really knew me.

But life had other idears,

My face got pocked,

I died many deaths looking into mirrors,

The doors to my sad kingdom utterly locked.

Still looking around for that strange smell,

It must be coming from under the sink,

I been sleeping in the inkwell,

I can only wonder what you must think.

...these floors creak like sick trolls in the dank darkness...
they know where we live, where we go to retrieve the
cosmic necessities, of certain talcums and oils and
balms, for your shadings in the mirror...you are
looking at yourself before your death, the moment
when your heart is whooshing red blood through the
micro-miles, and old lamps in moldy tearooms refuse
to stay lit, and now, young girls enter with skirts
ablaze...showing fauna and flora...

Word Lyric For Music #3
"Finding Repast at the Front Door"

Melissa and her sister are on the floor,

Dancing in circles without shoes, as before,

Dancing like tomorra' might not shine,

Sipping white whales and bottles of red wine,

They were seeking a brace of yes men, heretofore,

Now they're finding repast at the front door.

Older dudes with cigarettes dangling,

Said no with wives in tow;

Melissa and her sister stopped angling,

And found the limbo stick set down low,

They begged Tired Ed not to lower it anymore,

Now they're finding repast at the front door.

Late night promises made with a glass of rum,

Melissa's sister dancing to a delirious drum;

She's beckoning the boys to get down low,

And with wives in tow, as before,

The old dudes and Tired Ed got down on the floor,

But Melissa and her sister, heretofore,

Were finding repast at the front door.

...there is no sound here...only the wind blowing to the west...the ghosts of Truman and Nell peek through the windows of the old Santa Fe depot...they see Herb Clutter getting off the train in 1959...returning from an eastern sojourn... they follow him to the parking lot, whispering warnings to him..."Move away...take your family and move away...now...before it is too late..."

Word Lyric for Music #4
"Hearing the Wind in Garden City"

Got off the train at silent midnight,

Standing in the glow of a swerving streetlight,,

Then I heard something fly through the center of my soul,

It was the big yellow bird with black nuns in tow,

One by one the avenger attacked without pity,

But I was alone, hearing the wind in Garden City.

Drove on old Highway 50 at noon time,

Pulled the car into the shade with the Sinclair sign,

Standing in the darkness of the dour men's room,

I saw the Cherokee killer wearing the lizard costume,

Soon, seven miles down the highway, he will show no pity,

But I was alone, hearing the wind in Garden City.

Creeping slowly down the old oak lane,

I saw the house, and the green unforgotten pain,

The guys tied up the moon and left the sun afright,

And shot four holes through the heart of the night.

Then I heard something fly through the center of my soul,

It was the big yellow bird with black nuns in tow,

One by one the avenger attacked without pity,

But I was alone, hearing the wind in Garden City.

Standing over their graves in the shadows of Valley View,

I saw Nancy dancing in red, with Bobby dressed in blue,

I saw a terrified girl in the darkness, begging for her life,

I saw the guys carrying a blue-barreled shotgun, and a hunting knife.

There is blood on the walls, and innocence is lost,

Four ambulances on the lawn, their tracks are star-crossed,

Then I heard something fly through the center of my soul,

It was the big yellow bird with black nuns in tow,

One by one the avenger attacked without pity,

But I was alone, hearing the wind in Garden City.

Word Lyric #5 for Music
"Wishing for Another Wish"

Been wishing for the end of succumbing spring,

Now counting the days to begin a summer fling,

Wishing for a new start as time rounds the bend,

I have red roses and white wine packed to send.

I'm sitting in the crow's nest at journey's end.

Try not to breathe loud as we struggle to finish,

Sliding my suspicions to the other side of the dish,

As usual, I'm wishing for another wish.

Been wishing for an end to the usual thing,

But I'm dancing now and dying to sing,

Been working long everyday and stressin.'

I'm hoping and praying for your silent blessin'

As we glide from our table and across the floor,

Gonna dance tonight until walkin' out the door,

Try not to breathe loud as we struggle to finish,

Sliding my suspicions to the other side of the dish,

As usual, I'm wishing for another wish.

Been wishing for an end to suffocating summer,

Now I'm waiting for my Mississippi belle, to come here,

By bus in September she arrive's with empty purse,

From far and near, many cities and towns, quite diverse,

But I'm in love with this beauty from Biloxi,

My shady naughty lady with a ton of moxie.

Try not to breathe loud as we struggle to finish,

Sliding my suspicions to the other side of the dish,

As usual, I'm wishing for another wish.

Word Lyric #6 for Music
"You Could Hypnotize Someone"

Turn away your blinking blue eye,
It is searing my brain with wind and sky,
We are at pause here in this fountain of mystery,
We are standing here to reset the pulse of history,
Your rolling turning eye is silently sucking me in,
It cannot possibly change what might have been,
It is capturing my sadness, and stealing my soul away,
Please turn your blinking blue eye away, I say.
Like looking down the barrel of a burping gun,
There is no doubt, you could hypnotize someone.

Oh quiet lady, cast away your scary stares,
Into far-away space, beyond all chants and prayers.
Turn away your blinking blue orb from my sight,
It is draining my heaving convulsing body outright.
The weary world stumbles ahead drunk with wine,
Please quiet lady, turn, turn toward the sunshine.
We are at pause here in this fountain of mystery,
We are standing here to reset the pulse of history,
Like looking down the barrel of a burping gun,
There is no doubt, you could hypnotize someone.

...through the wooden front door, through the old screen door masked with bluesy gray memories...into the front room with the beige shag under our feet...into the arched dining room, with chandelier dangling...a right turn down the aged hallway, draped in birchwood, a light fixture above at the elbow, and a bedroom beyond...the lavatory with green and black clouds in the tiles, to the left...with Death on the black tiled floor...lying inert before the white sink... down the hall further...go left into the bedroom with the multi-rivered ceiling...28 cracks, and we lost count... estuaries through time and destiny...

Word Lyric #7 for Music
"It Isn't Far To the Dance Floor"

Mister Sinew is just standing still,

By the old phone booth on Pine Street.

He was curb-walking, looking for a thrill,

Now he is stopped, looking for place to eat.

Into Clyde's Café he casually saunters,

Mister Sinew in shark skin, with dark Melissa in chains,

She looks like a fish flopping out of the waters,

Mister Sinew is up to his old games.

Garçon! Garçon! A table for two please,

There, by the blinking neon light above the door,

 Seat us there, in the cool cross breeze,

And it isn't far to the dance floor.

Two hard cocktails with shrimp hors d'oeuvre please,

And add a nip of rum, to put Melissa on her knees,

But memories of Sister Mary Daniel returns to his brain

And her monotone warnings of his coup de main.

So Mister Sinew tells Melissa to get up from there, off the floor,

And quickly he scoots her out through the back door.

"Hey Ma! I was only lusting for a white whore,
And sweet Melissa went running out my back door!"

Into the traffic tangled throbbing,
Sweet Melissa goes a-bobbing,
Bobbing from every avenue and every confused street,
Looking for anyone dangerous she might meet.

But danger lurks in a '63 Ford four-door,
Bang! goes sweet Melissa, hit with guts flying galore,
Mister Sinew pulls up in this loud rod with exhaust spewing,
He walks over to her and asks "what are you doing?"

Unable to speak or breathe or be understood,
Sweet Melissa, in sections scattered, here and there,
Answered the best she could,
"I'm dead. Can't you see? I am up here in the air!

Garçon! Garçon! A table for two please,
There, by the blinking neon light above the door,
Seat us there, in the cool cross breeze,
And it isn't far to the dance floor.

"...never mind the dead flowers...and the beige coffin...I have them in my house to remind me that the Eternal Dude is ever near...look, they are all grandmothers now, with skin creases and wrinkles above flabby arms and drooping man dreams...are you awake girl?... never mind...sleep on, it takes me a half hour to reset..."

Word Lyric #8 for Music
"Living Ain't Breathing"

Never mind the dead flowers, and the beige coffin,

We all sit here and eat burnt popcorn quite often.

We lie around and pretend we're alive and kicking,

No sense in moving; we already gave life a good licking.

Now we play games in the darkness by the candle light,

We seek momentary bliss in the shadows of the numbing night

We peer and squint and gaze at the dirt from above,

We squirm motionless inside ourselves like a melting dove.

The dead around us are forever speechless in their wreathing,

They blink madly at the thought, that living ain't breathing.

Never mind the drooping ferns, and the open coffin,

I have been sitting here, and dry heaving, quite often.

I just hang around and pretend I'm okay, though alive,

The dead cannot hear me; their pleas I cannot revive.

My soul reposes there, inside the bronze cushioned box,

As the face of my eternal love, though dead, still talks.

Escape is worthy from the endless flow of days and nights,

From the forever glow of a million incandescent lights,

The dead around us are forever speechless in their wreathing,

They blink madly at the thought, that living ain't breathing.

Word Lyric #9 for Music
"Testimonies of Old Hippies"

We are still traveling by the speed of mind,

We're the old freaks, and survivors of the great Be In,

Winsome hippie girls, now old and still kind,

Play pan flutes with feathers glued to their skin.

We were there when Joe and Jimi stole the big show,

With their mythic renderings cast in vinyl stone,

What was it? Where are we? We did not exactly know,

Janis and Pete and Alvin Lee lacerated the night alone.

And we heard The Bear boogie on down the wooded road.

Some of us saw magic mushrooms smiling on a giant toad.

Richie Havens and Carlos Santana let it all fly as we sat there,

Far away into mind space, their epic explosions resounded,

Electric guitar hysterics with screaming rants compounded,

We were all laid to waste there, in the rock n' roll blare.

We old freaks still travel by the speed of mind,

Old dudes, and hippie girls hang around and are still kind,

We still secretly toke at midnight, all of us with the ghosts,

Of Joe and Jimi, when they sliced the sky, before that vast host.

Word Lyric #10 for Music
"Going To Walmart to Find Jesus"

Living in the fast lane is getting me down,

I worry about money, and am near a mental breakdown.

Debts are mounting and we're heading for war,

I don't trust the newspapers and the government anymore.

But I know God almighty is up there and he sees us,

I'm going to Walmart to find Jesus!

Am parking my car in the crowded lot,

Other Walmarters are coming out with what they bought.

Carrying bags and boxes filled with salvation and joy,

After standing in endless lines designed to annoy.

But I know God almighty is up there and he sees us,

I'm going to Walmart to find Jesus!

Am following this lady with tight skirt and no bra,

Surely with a build so robust and firm she hasn't a flaw.

But her basket is filled with bitterness and hate,

It is this way, from city to city, and state to state.

But I know God almighty is up there and he sees us,

I'm going to Walmart to find Jesus!

Am watching this dude with tattooes test-tasting the grapes,

I wonder from how many prisons he planned his escapes.

Now I realize he is like all the rest of us, Americans out to survive,

Struggling everyday from sunrise to sunset to stay alive.

But I know God almighty is up there and he sees us,

I'm going to Walmart to find Jesus!

Now I'm scanning my entire life with visa credit card in hand,

First come the frozen things, then all the fools I can't stand.

Ringing up the total for all that my existence depends on,

Now I'm paying the balance for another golden dawn.

But I know God almighty is up there and he sees us,

I'm going to Walmart to find Jesus!

My Dead Beating Heart

There is no dishonor

In telling the earth to remain silent.

We pilgrims will sit stoically

In the genuflecting shade,

And breathe in the seething exhalations

Of this diseased planet;

Trays of sweet prunes and tangerines

Will be brought in,

And girls with red lips and ringed fingers

Will bend to feed us.

Volumes of Plato will be dispersed,

And dancers with diamonds

Will frolic to the loud contusions

Of a fast-moving summer storm.

They will scream bloody curses

Into the thin clasps of the Republic,

With staggering fusillades,

Enveloping everything real and not real,

Everything a dead man could want,

All within shouting sprays of anger.

And the lost girls, scores of them,

Half naked and convulsing,

Will bend over for the piercing prongs

Of pleasure and pain; two dudes,

Set to penetrate

With spasmodic ejaculations, into

The thin steel curtain of fear,

The biting teeth of confusion.

We pilgrims know where

To find death on a platter.

We know how to mix

The batter of desire with fresh dalliances;

All of it entwined and tied up,

With grasping snap dragons

Dressed in wheezing mauve.

The doors on the south side,

Of this old ruined mansion,

Lead to the tulip gardens;

Where the dry hard mud of lost time

Finds no pause in its moist dominations;

You and I will embrace in the rain there,

As it was, that long-ago day in 1971,

When our quivering lips sought new glories,

Celebrating our insatiable embraces of arousal-

When the gods of passion were first created!

And epic wars were never lost!

There is no dishonor

In being buried in the final earth.

No penalty can be spoken of

By silent corpses in a sleeping graveyard.

The skeletons know too many secrets,

Which they whisper about, shhh…

In ghostly intonations…

Spoken with the night wind…

Of muted weeping and whimpering episodes,

With writhing virgin girls,

And empty kleenex boxes… on the side table.

The two yapping dogs downstairs

Can smell this disease, up here,

And as sure as this troubled earth turns,

They will escape their loving master yet,

Just to sniff my dead beating heart!

Forbidden Chocolate

I was riding psychedelic,

Riding Electric Ladyland,

Inside

The long wheezing worm,

Riding easy,

Through the black snoring night,

Aboard the Amtrak Southwest Chief,

Roaring and rumbling,

Down the track for distant Kansas,

Heading east,

To silent Garden City.

I had donned white earbuds in Barstow,

Connected umbilically,

To my ITunes universe,

And stoned as Hendrix himself,

On forbidden chocolate,

I rode in the windowed lounge car

At midnight,

Observing the vast darkness of America,

At 90 miles an hour.

As Jimi dazzled me with Voodoo Child,

From 1968,

On his white Fender stratocaster,

I saw before me,

The imploding annihilation of the universe,

With passing strobe-light torpedoes,

Pelting my mind like exploding hail stones;

The distant country lights flying by,

And through me,

In a whirring surreal-like blur.

I was riding psychedelic,

Riding Electric Ladyland,

Inside

The long wheezing worm,

Riding easy,

Through the black snoring night,

Across the California expanse

Of wind and sand and stars;

Across the rich pallets

Of Arizona and New Mexico,

The upper tranquil reaches

Of southern Colorado;

The high flat Kansas plains,

Listening to Jimi tear apart the world

Like a rampaging Godzilla,

Coming into Tokyo with his fiery axe!

I saw colors and shadows,

And strange tracings out there,

Flickering like swamp bugs

In the dry darkness,

Aboard the Amtrak Southwest Chief,

Roaring and rumbling,

Down the track for distant Kansas,

Heading east,

To silent Garden City.

The Finest Destinations

Open the picture album now.

Clasped in fake gold with plastic ridges,

It is stunningly old, and yellowing;

An odorous time machine,

Filled with ancient heartbeats,

Frozen in the unstoppable hour,

Like grave stones in the snow.

Look at page one, leaning there,

The sixteen year old Mexican girl,

With the tanned, inward turning legs.

She dances with bare feet in the darkness.

She slides along the cool floor in the suave shadows.

I remember her ripening voice from decades ago,

Whispering muted words of tentative devotion,

Holding a rosebud in the unreal garden, as

Searching fingers found the finest destinations,

The incredible perfumed places,

Sealed in wax,

Scrolled as with papyrus,

Our secret intimacies finding ballast,

In repeated late night groans, with

Heaving spectacular ingestions,

Before an insatiable eating fire,

Our gaping mouths engorged,

With mad tongues of lapping astonishments.

Close the picture album now.

Haven't you had enough?

Inside A '72 Econoline

This old green van has a musty smell to it,

Like a pair of sweaty rancid socks

Mixed with half-empty beer cans.

It's a banged up thing, this '72 Econoline.

Scratches and mysterious dents

Cover its façade,

Like boils on a hairless mastodon.

A spare tire rests under the torn carpet,

Bearing testimonies of premeditated audacities.

But it's a clean driving machine,

This green econoline,

As it glides loudly, unnoticed

Under the ubiquitous stars.

Music by Townsend and Daltry

Assaults our senses with barbed bullets,

Sent outward and beyond electric space,

Like teenage belches lost forever

Within a forgotten alcoholic haze.

And there we were, she and I

Surviving, as victims of desire,

Our naked statuary embedded,

With perfumed skin and green blood,

And we, then pure and free,

Cried hysterically and uncontrollably,

Inside a wilting wasteland

Of dark and desperate pleadings.

"Hey, I like your eyes,

And the touch of your skin.

Let's cozy up here.

We can hold on to each other

On top of this foul shag.

Victor's Econoline smells bad,

Don't ya think?

Soon we'll be sleeping on the sand,

And breathing fresh air again."

She is the silly blue-eyed blond

From the higher-up back hills.

He is the skinny laughing dog

From the lower-down flat lands.

Their caressing fingers

Now silently disappear,

Under enveloping layers

Of rayon, nylon and polyester,

Hiding their blood-crazed probings,

Inside the '72 Econoline,

As it glides loudly, unnoticed

Under the ubiquitous stars.

"Press your thumb against mine now.

Let's mesh our dirty minds

Into one remarkable embrace;

Shhh, silence now,

No words are needed."

Rubbing flesh here and there,

Atop their striped beach towel,

Ensconced in the dank darkness,

The skinny dog and the silly blond

Find tortured bliss

With groping fondness,

While breathing and stirring

As one rolling organism,

Plied to remain motionless,

In the emasculating upheavals

Of bootleg love; they remain

In constant retrograde,

Their consuming margins of ascendance,

Seeking and spiraling there,

Like flowered temple dancers on fire!

We must ask,

"Will it play in Peoria?

What is it about your empty gazes,

Your nothing stares,

That are as dry as the wind at noon?

Shh, you don't have to say a word.

You don't have to say anything at all."

This old green van stinks to highest heaven,

And Victor knows this,

But nothing is to be done about it.

Nothing.

His sweaty socks will stay put here.

Those beer cans will rest easy for another six months.

The days and nights of 1973 will roll on by,

Inexorably so, and

This '72 Econoline will continue to spew out

Outrageous odors,

As it glides loudly, unnoticed

Under the ubiquitous stars.

Blind Hearses

Another dubious nuptial at sundown,

Sequestered beyond the rolling tribal hills,

South of Spring Street across the bridge,

Down the road aways, maybe seven miles.

Another ceremony of spoken vows and tears,

Hidden carefully to the thorny south,

Behind myriad grape vines all around,

That lasso in the shadowed evenings of August,

With their ripened essences and moistened residue,

Breathe it all in now, this perfumed evening of lights,

Sifting into your nostrils, with no sound at all,

Except, shhh, do you hear those shrill voices in the distance?

Can you hear their wine glasses tinkling

And clinking, like melting ice in a sober shade?

Blind hearses travel this way all the time now,

Black and white and beige hearses,

All seeking a crossroad in the swallowing fog,

Carrying more astonished corpses,

Dressed in ruined starched finery,

Wearing nothing smiles carved like pumpkins,

Down the side avenues leading to the Shadow,

To the newly dug graves in the sunlight.

A chorus of fools will enter inside the back way,

As they have for decades of lost time;

They will come to chant mournful dirges

Into the non-listening, soul-stricken night.

As again, one of their own, finds the Shadow,

And the darkened avenue, with muted footsteps.

Where Has All The Beauty Gone?

There is no time like the now times,

The ever-present blood-swooshing times.

Time again to surrender as a smitten lover surrenders,

To the never-ending rhapsodies of erotic impulses,

Which exhale as a listless leviathan exhales,

Basking in the swishing waters off the windy capes,

Naked, but kept hidden, in the unknown anterior rooms,

Of a hundred dark mansions in the draping hollows,

Encased with ethereal atmospheres and essences,

In stony gold, glittering emeralds, and smooth diamonds,

All dazzling the senses with spurting explosions of light,

Of helpless exaltations and cooing astonishments;

Now they're seeking the old nights and the old embraces

In the gaping moonlight, amid intense and timid arousals;

Their blinking black eyes squinting from behind the papered
walls,

Of dustless airless rooms with drooping statues of dead poets,

Alive still as they rise again in mythic intonations,

Making suave movements with pointing soft fingers,

Upon the moist nape of blond submitting desires.

Watching in spirit now as they once peeped at lovers;

Peeping and prying and peering from behind infinitesimal holes,

Never seen before by the living or the bereaved,

Nor by the delirious or the unjustly defamed;

Now they just bite us, the souls of the dead boys in blue.

And they watch us from behind those bare walls,

Those breathing twitching snarling walls.

So, where has all the beauty gone?

Covered Dishes

1

The password is… password, shhh…
Try to remember if possible,
this sure-fire way of getting through the door;
Entering indeed, as with all lithesome ladies,
and their dithering dogs, after
entreating the big dude at the entrance gate,
with licorice sticks and cauliflower juice on ice,
and leaning over long enough to show off the planets,
those spinning orbs of a mathematical universe,
now turning madly and centrifugally, sucking
out the eyes of the pleading fools,
dressed in rage, and wont to feel the ancient eclipses,
those silent but grunting interludes unseen,
all dressed in satin boredom, all flummoxed
as with clowns, dressed in neon failure,
who now offer smiles and winking winces,
to the sad-eyed pedestrians, and
the red-lipped ladies with the wide-brimmed hats,
out to tease with nylon exposures,
around the bleakly lighted doorways
to dark entrances, without eyes to feel.

You were sitting there with legs crossed,

a cocktail dangling from your frozen fingertips,

like a fainted ballerina in the splitting moonlight.

In front of you, on the table, covered dishes

covered tureens, with surprise taste delights simmering,

shouting out in mute languages of the multitudes:

What is under the lid of this blue dish?

What is beneath the cover of this steaming tureen?

I turned to see other dishes and other culinary settings,

and instead, I saw you among the bon bons

and the flaming surrendering soufflé.

You wore that same translucent skirt with

the lightning stripes and the chiffon protestations,

and as you rose from your chair with howling legs,

there was no hell and brimstone in what I saw.

Then as with a silent hungry leopard,

setting exotic eyes on my stilled soul and quivering body,

you took my hand into yours, as easily as one might,

and with straight-staring certitude, we politely exited

from this quiet pedestrian grille,

this obscure café under the yawning stars,

hidden behind festooning flowers,

draped on hungry trellises,

for the hopelessly outraged.

2

Into the tattooed tavern
we sauntered dreamily,
squinting our delirious eyes, while
blinking rapidly, and flinching from
the electronic glare of spit-polished mirrors,
shining as an insane sun would,
without reflection, without resonance,
hanging on a purple breast, extending out
like a promontory of covered platters and purple dishes;
and there were young girls present
wearing the costumes of the naked,
seeking to dance in the germ puddles,
with waxed earbuds donned,
and eyes scanning
for blue jean bulges, a promise, and a ring.
Instead, they find the Shadow,
pulsating wildly under the neon cocktail
that oozes desperation;
they crisscross the floor, only
to find more phony friends, and traipsing ghosts
that hurry away, never looking, never listening.
"Ah, miss, may I buy you a white whale?

Certainly I can afford to buy you

a moment of pointless romance."

But she doesn't perceive the wondrous latitude,

of that amazing moment in time,

this hollowed babe in black heels,

just staring point blank into my eyes.

Waiting for the nod,

the supreme tilt to aggrandizement!

At last it arrives, as autumn sensibly arrives,

and the truth can be seen.

"I would kiss you now, miss,

here under this humming cocktail sign,

that glows its neon blood

upon your open lips. But

Death wants another drink. Look.

It's waiting down the bar a ways.

It's staring at you with mouth decidedly open;

It wants your blood in a beer glass,

with your sea-sodden tears in a chaser."

3

Your sullen muted whispers,

wafting in this dank whiskey inn,

are falling on wide-open ears, except,

your mousey annoying voice lacerates my brain

with claws that rip and tear and impale,

yet, I desire more of this, here

with these wet unhappy sots,

lost forever like me,

on a dark numbing cloud,

as it floats aimless to the endless east,

leeward like a restless barge,

netting and trapping more broken souls,

more reluctant denizens, more

lodgers for the vacant harbor inns,

and the laurel-shaded graveyards.

But we are different than they, you and I.

We know when to stop talking,

and start nodding.

"Miss, could you speak up, I can't hear you."

The din of these dozens of voices here,

amongst these dancing grabbing fools,

are drowning out your sad pleadings.

But I can taste your sadness, and your

self-realization of a life worth nothing.

"I'm lost and don't know where to turn."

Then, in the neon darkness,

the staid barkeep places a covered porcelain dish

on our corner table, by the exit sign,

brimming and teeming furiously

with steamed remonstrances of insatiable fear.

"You should see me in the morning," she says,

"Certainly not now, when it is the end of day,"

when night has ascended its ego curtain,

and a thousand imperfections are revealed.

"No, not now!"

"But my dear," I say, with eyes screwed forward,

"You are perfect in the twilight time,"

this now time, as we sit here in the back booth,

sipping these strong white whales.

"No! you fool of a man!" she says,

"I am not perfect enough!"

"**...way up there,** I see the shadow, and the endless...turning..."

...these deceased still lurk there, eating from empty
bowls and bare dishes...the chandelier still hangs in
musty cobwebs, with the ghostly lights of 1967 still
emanating from the outside; but down that hallway...
the 9 year old boy heard someone, or a strange sound,
that day in 1961, while alone in the house...a loud
creaking sound from a heavy footstep...on the green
carpeted hallway...by the thermostat; he stood to see
what was there...nothing, just another ghost from past
days, when heartbreak visited that morning in May,
down the hallway...shhh...there is someone stepping
down the hallway...turn right at the elbow...past the
green tiled shower room, the black tiled death floor...
and now...on the right...the largest bedroom...with
reflecting mirrors, and a dead man under a blanket...
these deceased ghosts still lurk there...still eating from
empty bowls and bare dishes...

III. Scenes From the Declive

Catholic

Stern but saintly Father Meissen

scolded the parents for not having

their baby boy baptized sooner.

It was April, 1952,

inside the stained-glassed catholic church,

ensconced on sun-split Newlin street,

avenue of pink oleanders and cracking sidewalks.

According to the chagrined mother,

she was told that delaying this pivotal sacrament

for three complacent months,

after the boy's birth on January 11,

was unequivocally unacceptable,

and that waiting so eternally and unendingly,

actually jeopardized her befuddled baby's soul.

For if he had died, say in March of 1952,

unbaptized,

then his eternal soul, because of original sin,

would have been mercilessly subject

to the inscrutable tortures of hell,

and the lake of fire.

As per destiny, this glued-on scenario

was not realized, and instead,

the boy received the abundant graces

of a head-turning God that day,

as the boy's shiny oblivious head

was gently and sanctimoniously doused

with priestly-blessed holy water, fresh

from the rippling baptismal fount,

anchored dogmatically with rusted rebar,

deep below the shadowy sacristy,

among the obstinate urns

and the dark-voiced Dominus vobiscums.

But now we hear his older, wiser voice,

undulating like a lark's-heel after the begging,

hiding the treason of a reprobate mind,

fondling the prayers of ten thousand children,

crying silent astonished tears

into the cold marble baptismal fount;

A groping wet madness firmly set

among the kneeling statues, and the holy linens,

encrusted with fool's gold and trusting threads.

What kept these stilled voices unheard for so long?

Why did they not speak before this somber time?

Why did they bend, roll over and

close their eyes so cooperatively?

So reverently?

No one can possibly speak

about the unspeakable, for

Father's holy, righteous indulgences

were unequivocally unacceptable.

But it is too late now.

Mine eyes can clearly see now

the crying sunken skull at Golgotha,

turning its furious eyes away.

"...there is no turning, when you look away, towards me…"

Under This Azure October Sky

Still cruising here,

Still hunkering here

under this azure October sky

Still breathing here,

Still suffocating here,

inside this hair dryer which covers my head.

Still surviving here,

Still perspiring here,

outside, in the mad hot jungle called life.

Still riding here,

Still traveling here,

through all these lingering avenues

of time-spent days,

the remembering boulevards of months,

the forgetting hi-ways of years.

Still moving here,

through these wild inexorable hours,

of devouring events and digesting memories,

of searching for the unobtainable,

somewhere, inside a forgotten chest,

containing nothing.

Still traveling here,

Still traipsing here,

into the busy peopled shops

where the living never look into your eyes.

Still digesting here,

Still listening here,

to the final words of the wise ones,

the superior ones, the dead ones.

Still dreading here,

the final breath, the final heartbeat,

the climaxing stare, the last look.

Still cruising here,

Still riding fast into the tunnel of love.

Still missing here,

old ghostly friends, some gone to the grave,

some gone the way of the wind's druthers.

Still missing the dead here,

all swallowed into the breath of the wind,

digested in an instant of collapsing time.

Still riding low here,

Still kicking back here,

under this azure October sky.

...I see dead people behind those old comatose windows... they lurk there, staring out at us, the living. "hey, got a smoke?" "who is that speaking?" "we dead."

Your Long Angular Feet

You don't know me, but

I been riding here in this trundling lounge car

for two hours now, watching

you and your long angular feet,

while rumbling over these burdened tracks,

to silent Garden City, up there in Kansas

on the high wheat plains, sky bound!

I been wondering what your name is.

Alas, it is really none of my business,

but your silent intuitive look,

your expressive knowing gaze,

has intrigued me with repentant ambivalences, and

guilty acknowledgements within my mind,

far beyond any understandable explanation,

far beyond the passing distant New Mexico mountains,

as they inertly move with silent dogged violence,

out there, in the whirring passing blur,

beyond these curving airy Amtrak eyes,

of blue tint and orange penetrating glare,

wrought with distorting apparitions of yellow

and green wheezing monsters of morning light,

with the Super Chief masticating eastern miles,

like a termite boring ferociously, slashing

into the railroad ties of unyielding time;

And so we sit, staring out this bubble window in the sun,

and I been wondering about you.

I been believing you're educated, I can tell,

by the look of your pursed lips,

indicative of past heartbreaks and meltdowns;

and I been believing you're a democrat,

by your descending, unhearing stare,

indicative of past arguments with fools

who sleep near obelisks, set in old stone.

And as you gaze far away

through the lounge car windows,

deep into New Mexico, its heart and rocky soul,

I wonder what you're remembering there,

smiling, at peace with your intended purpose.

It was really nothing to me or anyone else,

nothing earth-shaking or profoundly circumstantial,

but you got off in Albuquerque,

you and your long angular feet,

and you walked away, like a dead person

in an old film reel.

...these are dead dudes now...they never grew old like us...
we always said as old men we would sit around and listen
to our music...and now we are old, the last leaves off the
tree, repeating winter annihilations have brought us
here...we live on.

In My Dappled Dream I Saw You

In my dappled dream I saw you,

Your shimmering ghost, young again,

As we were, when soft flares hid your brown legs,

There, in the warm April shadows, us

Astride an old beach blanket on the grass of Corona.

1971 was sensational when we were 19 years old;

We held each other like lovers afoul in the neutral shade,

And kissed deeply there, as ants found crumbs of cookies,

Laid there by swishing palms in the dishonest sunlight.

Oh lady, it was madness most discrete, indeed,

behind the boyfriend's back, miles away to the east;

You found new passions in our discretions there,

You delivered moist messages with muted giggles there.

Oh lady, you were wildly untrue to him that day!

Rolling as young leopards at play,

Our lips found its prey with mindless precision,

There, in the afternoon spectacle of leering light,

Of young lovers deliberately cheating,

Tendering desperate embraces in the perfumed shadows.

...see the screen door, behind the '59 Chevy Impala?...
behind it, in the gray darkness...she and I did the dance
of electric night...we saw many shadowy creatures on
the walls there, sought numerous paths for a light source
there...saw the stars from our backs, looking through the
transparent screen door at silent midnight...saw other
esoteric episodes there ...1967... I remember you, as one
who once walked by me, like a flirting ghost, in a
forgotten graveyard...

Sizzling Surprises

I'm ruminating here on this promenade of sizzling surprises.

I'm sitting here, watching the living denizens walk on by.

None of these sentient beings ever look at me,

Never see or acknowledge me, not for one second,

Never say even one word to me, as I sit half dead here,

On this hardened beaten park bench.

Just watching and wondering why the heck they don't look at me.

Ah, there's a young lady, just sat down across from me,

On the bench over there, a dozen purposeful strides away.

Hey honey, look over here. I'm an old dude still walking the earth;

You know, like you and everyone else; I'm just looking at you,

I mean no harm, really. Just checking you out, as a half-dead man would,

Desperately, with no conscience or inward analysis.

Just looking at your slender svelte legs, crossed like pretzels in the sun,

And I am thinking and wondering why you don't look at me.

Is it because I'm an old dude, with one foot in the grave?

Is it because you're afraid to encounter another human being, face to face?

A human who has seen the fortunes and misfortunes of a long life.

A human man who can create a masterpiece of sizzling surprises,

Just for you, all in a matter of five astonishing minutes!

Oh, for God's sake!

Stop staring at your cellphone and look over here, just for ten seconds!

I'm an old dude still walking the earth,

And I could teach you a thing or two about living,

About connecting and responding and empathizing,

About turning your mono-vision away from yourself, and your narcissism.

Just for ten seconds, try to see the loneliness of another sentient being;

You know, like me and everyone else here; I'm just looking at you,

I mean no harm, really. Just want to connect, as I once did with the young ladies,

Long ago under this same sizzling sun, up there,

Long ago when I sought those same sizzling surprises that I seek now,

And the sucking maelstrom of intense pleasures I could conjure up for you,

All in a matter of five astonishing minutes!

"...young men then...seeking the circles of smoke and liquids...it was summer twilight time, 1976, with sinister shadows and clutching branches nearby...it was imperceptible...the incessant turning of shapes and sounds, of liquid life, avalanching us, astonishing us, with the wild turnings of this ride; we intuitively knew the road ahead was paved with sadness..."

Crescent Time Breathing

There is no reach by which we as breathing creatures of crescent time,

Can ascertain the crouching intentions behind an elm tree with acorn outbursts,

Designed to scan the visions of the seething statues which stand upright in dark halls,

There is no grasping the dog tail complacencies by which we as mandrakes can navigate,

The crest-line urgencies behind drawn curtains which beggars a pittance of mild regret,

Absorbed obsessively with intense window flashings at noon with skin and lace,

3 o'clock connivances wearing nothing but a wistful grin seeking summits of perfumed ice,

There is no reach by which any living contrivance can mock the wags of crescent time,

We are ridiculous in our incessant acorn outbursts designed to scan the farthest atom.

"...And nothing may come to your mind, nothing at all, just empty space, a lot of dust, some shadows, there, in the corner.... some boxes that have nothing in them, a lamp with the lamp light that doesn't work, and the curtains that hang down have holes in them. You can see some spiderwebs inside of them, but only dead spiders clinging to the ancient threads. There's a chair with a little pillow on it. What personage sat there and when? By the window there is a light, a kerosene lamp, it is always lit, day and night, it is lit, as with a vestal fire, behind that shrouding curtain, on a table by a chair, the chair with the pillow. Nothing. Nothing is there. Nothing in my mind except maybe a nebulous memory, yet still there like some old statuary, the sight of that girl, the one in red who did nothing to help me that day, when she said goodbye. Nothing is how I felt. Nothing. The strawberries out back, lounging in the sunlight, like bleeding eggs, beckon the warm grasping touch of the girl. Just seek the pathway that leads around into the shadows, to the back where the strawberries cling, growing, proliferating wildly, passionately, energetically all over the dead land, the vegetation just oozing with dirt, completely swallowing me as I slide down the hole..."

Like Cool Hand Luke

They put me inside the Box.

Like Cool Hand Luke, they did.

A long night inside the Box in the dark;

Off yonder I can hear the hounds a baying.

Ostracized from the inside group,

The inclusive cool cloud of friends, and rightly so.

They put me inside the Box for having a backbone.

Like Cool Hand Luke, they did.

Treating me like a dead man,

With no memory, heartbeat or name,

Just a dead dude, cast away like a detested rock,

Thrown to the dark part of the back garden,

To make clear for the new trees, and rightly so.

They put me inside the Box, for having a backbone.

Like Cool Hand Luke, they did.

I sit alone and pray now,

And wait for the approaching footsteps,

And the jangling of certain keys outside my locked door.

Have pity on me Boss! I promise not to talk no more!

They put me inside the Box.

Like Cool Hand Luke, they did.

A long night inside the Box in the dark.

Off yonder I can hear the hounds a baying.

"...in the tuft of distant shade, there is the continuous throbbing of electric heartbeats, as seeking attendant spirits hide behind invisible eyes, lurking with sad stories to tell that no one has heard; all these alive spirits here can see us, as we wonder how it is when the breathing stops...listen....they are whispering something that no human seems to understand... there is no death..."

Suburban Mindmelt

You and I know what it takes to make the sky turn around.

We still know when to stop in our tracks,

To look and smell and pause; we must, if we can,

For we are sad souls in a suburban mindmelt;

We know the numbers but not the rules of return.

We must daily continue on and go our wearisome ways,

Opening metal doors to various offices,

Housed with experts we pay to rid our lives of the various afflictions and maladies,

Acquired in divers ways, during esoteric transactions,

Privately and publicly exchanged, apportioned properly and lawfully,

before dinners in dark dives, with candle-lit apparitions traipsing on the walls,

and ketchup bottles jostling in the middle of large tables.

We have seen the stars, mad as dancers twirling sur les pointes in the dark.

We have seen them startle us with their consistent placements and positions.

We have heard the stoned sounds of a multitude of vibrating cymbals,

Slicing the suburban mindmelt, with the notes of mayhem, madness and redemption.

You and I now know what it takes to lock a door and turn out a light, just before midnight,

When the earth demons go on the prowl for lost faces and young sadness.

We know what it takes to change a record, or the sound of our voices at noon.

Be quiet as you speak when it is midday, for the fishmonger and his boy have big ears.

Be still and do not breathe.

You and I know what it takes to make the sky turn around,

For we are sad souls in a suburban mindmelt;

We know the numbers, but not the rules of return.

Hello Intrepid Reader of Poetry

Hello intrepid reader of poetry.

Nice of you to drop in.

I would offer you a diet soda,

And a few tokes of the ganja out in the garage,

but I am not there, and you aren't here; so that's that.

Nevertheless, this blank document is where I find substantial solace,

Away from the insane oozing organism,

Called Life, here in this fast-paced sojourn from point A to point B, alas

There is some truth lurking inside the small trivial things,

which tug at our sinking sanity, daily.

One hour after waking up,

we are planning dinner;

The highlight of another typical day.

But you, intrepid reader of poetry,

these are not your ways, nor your thoughts.

For you have significant work to accomplish,

important people to meet and enjoin;

Long books to read, and letters of importance to answer,

Then, another night of soft sleep to be had,

With dour dreams that never presage anything epic,

Never tasting anything with "sour misfortune's book,"

Although at times, we must wonder.

So, you like poets? Here is my card:

As you can see, I am just another word dandy and time traveler,

Walking and traipsing this amazing planet, like you,

Like all the others who found the Muse and lent an ear, but

Are we not of the same splendid gardens?

The same fountains east of the eucalyptus trees?

Are we not of the gentle immortals,

who soulfully now reside in the secret shadows?

Will you now walk with me down this still path.

To the back house, out amongst the ivy trellises swooning in silence?

So, are you still there my friend?

My intrepid reader of poetry?

Did my latest poetic plunge bore you beyond all human tolerance?

Did you just waste two minutes of your life that you will never get back,

while reading this forgettable attempt at poetry writing?

So, where is everyone going tonight?

Any parties? Any ladies looking for a little nookie in the dark?

Hello honey. Nice of you to drop in.

What do the clientele call you around here?

Hi Vixen, care for a diet soda?

...show these dead souls the way, their time has come and gone, long ago...back in 1967, they saw "Now" on their plates...and then, with the turning of the shadow...they finally saw themselves as the former ones...the late ones, whose fit is now long over...

"I see we have something to discuss...step inside this shell, and allow me the honor to show you what the multitudes have been wanting to see since the….turning of the Age…no, it won't harm you, or make any financial demands upon you…it just seeks…the shadow…" …a worn path to a garden tower…a descending ladder, and tinted windows, 15 feet up…plush velvet, and bison heads on the walls…"

To Be Ancient

It is good to be ancient,

As with a vintage of the eternal red,

Sealed for the duration with an aged English cork.

Now youthful impulses hold no sway in the empty offing.

I recall them all, as I have remembered certain dreams all my life,

Undead ghosts from distant tree-lined shores in time,

Strolling languorously in a marshy fetid fog;

Their ancient faces I remember caressing,

Their yearning eyes and doubting smiles I recall seeing,

And the supple lips of some I can still feel, recalling,

The passionate interspersed minutes of unreal time,

Secretly spent, behind concealing curtains and ascending ivy vines,

With no real words of crystalline memory being uttered or heard.

And now, returning from wet membranes hidden insidiously,

Inside the watery swooshing gullies inside my brain,

Old friends and lovers appear again, like in an old film,

As they meander an astonished ancient avenue in single file.

Look at these dead pale girls here!

Girls who once spiraled to the stars in the darkness!

Now they tiptoe by my front window, perfume-scented,

Seeking their simple tombstones in the far graveyard.

Screaming Guillotines

I.

I sit on the wide veranda of this house called America,

And I can see the Beast Boys coming our jungled way,

Coming like wild torrents of lapping flames over the astonished landscape,

Coming with black eyes squinting and staring for a feast of blood.

I sit trembling with mouth wide open, waiting for the whistling hearses to come,

And the inevitable silent tap upon my evading shoulder.

And far far away into the green enveloping expanse,

Of consuming trees and obliterating American skies,

I can hear the screaming guillotines serenading the ghost dancers.

I can see the whistling hearses bringing in the crimson nightmares.

II.

Time to take my knife again and lacerate the flesh of this dead thing,

This once-breathing creature that felt nothing but the slash of profit.

Time to spit out the long thin hairs entwined around my teeth.

Time to wonder whose hair this belongs to, as I pull out the long strands slowly,

Like pulling out long segmented worms from beneath the dirt of a rock.

"Ah, do you know the time? Is your sister coming by today?

She knows my name, and she can hear the screaming guillotines when they drop.

Will she spend some time with me here on my soft bumpy sofa?

Will she at last listen, at last hear, my remonstrances of lost love,

As we devour this dead, unbreathing thing,

Inside this salty steaming stew?"

III.

The Profit Boys are back in town,

And Jess and Jim are drunk on whiskey.

John Jupiter and his new bride, Isabel,

Are eating chicken and dumplings without a frown.

His new suit, in whisky-laden tatters, is

Hanging propped on a sweat-stained hall tree.

"Lordy those two are riling me; but shucks, it's my wedding day!"

Then into town rides the Domino Kid from Abilene;

He's looking to escape the screaming guillotines at Lansing.

John Jupiter and Isabel drink a toast to the future,

Their happy hearts pounding with hopeful glee;

Then he bashfully presents a wedding ring to his dimpled bride,

And kisses her sweetly under the tall Dragon tree.

But now, inside their barn, with soft lamplight aglowing,

Amidst the rambling rawhide, and a cracked cowbell,

Jess and Jim Profit set fire to the hayloft, a fire that is still growing;

The Domino Kid lies asleep, eternally dreaming of Isabel.

"...your long angular feet were resting there, in New Mexico... just what are you thinking about?...these strangers here are oblivious of what 's ahead...look out there! See it!"

The American Morning

We ride smoothly, deliberately, in this old cruising caravan,

Across the ancient American avenues and boulevards,

Of the once living, and now, the finally dead,

Of the once famous, and now, the finally forgotten;

Of tattooed memories applied in the American morning, cooking

In the back kitchen, with yellow-yoked eggs frying rapturously,

Like monstrous hoards of buzzing locusts, out to kill,

In black pans, sizzling and searing sensationally;

With mysterious, soulful realizations of disappearing time,

The heavenly odors of bacon fat, rising to the old-fashioned clouds,

We come here to turn the radio dial, in this summer of winning and losing;

But now it is all turning, turning as the shadows of life should turn,

For life is the now of when and why; and we all know now,

What 's waiting and lurking behind the curtained door.

"No, kind sir, you go first through the door, sir, if you please."

But as we ride now through these blighted snapshots in time,

This creeping caravan from the American morning comes to a halt.

Through the windshield and into the American night, old eyes see

A crowd of black ballplayers, gathering in Harlem on East River Avenue,

Looking to get inside the big ball yard, with the Babe, the Yankee Clipper,

And the Iron Horse, hitting fungoes over the EL station, over there,

Dressed in over-sized pinstripes, dripping in dirt and tobacco juice,

Tipping sweat-stained caps to the roaring, crescendoing ovations,

Thundering upward and through the airy reaches of the big ball yard,

Somehow do not reach their ears; still, they run fast, as if being chased,

Run faster than all the dead baseball gods of the American morning!

But now it is all turning, turning as the shadows of life should turn,

For life is the now of when and why; and we all know now,

What's waiting and lurking behind the curtained door.

"No, kind sir, you go first through the door, sir, if you please."

To See It With Open Eyes?

What is wrong with everyone?

Every time I turn around,

someone is accusing someone else of being a racist.

What is this racist thing?

Is it a disease of some kind? Does it bite?

You all sound like something slinking in the dark garden,

croaking and oozing there with the slimy toads and the rude crickets.

"Racist! …Racist!... Racist!"…

What creature is this that lurks so loudly in the wet weeds?

What vile manner is this, that makes a person wonder,

Will it kill me when it jumps out at me?

Will it bite me when I bend down close

to see it with open eyes?

"Racist! …Racist!... Racist!"…

What is this annoying debased thing,

which squirms and squishes loudly in the dark garden?

What repulsive grunt is this, that makes a person wonder,

Will it sting me when it lunges at me?,

Will it attack me when I bend down close

to see it with open eyes?

"Racist!... Racist!... Racist!"…

There it goes again, making that same irksome insane sound.

Will it ever cease? Will it ever just keel over, and die?

What is this racist thing?

Does it have a big drooling mouth with hungry teeth?

Is it some grotesque monster from far beneath

the surface of the earth?

I think… it stinks like something that's been dead for centuries.

"Racist!... Racist!... Racist!"…

What is wrong with everyone?

The Translucent Loft

The girls choir at St. Mary's still sing there.
Shh, be quiet as we step inside
through these green rectangular doors,
Shh! Listen...
We can hear them up there,
in the translucent loft.

They are still cloistered upstairs in the saintly glow,
of stained glass fortissimos, and bare knees,
dressed in blue sweaters with plaid beanies doffed
upon the three dozen crowns of the virgin sainted;
And now before us, the majesty of the holy sanctuary,
the deep eternity of ever-swallowing horizontal constictions,
upon which the devout might meditate the spirit mysteries,
with blessed rosaries, scapulars, and communion wafers,
bristling miraculously upon flaming tongues of fire.

"Shh! Be quiet here in the church, it is a sin to talk!"

We must fold our hands in silent contrition to an invisible
God.
We must say our prayers, memorized from old missals.
We must genuflect on bended leg, making the sign of the
cross.

But still, a likeness of our creator, dead and naked,

Nailed and bloody, with sickening thorns and gushing crimson,

hangs before us most ignominiously, a dead creator.

How can this be, Father Dawson?

Why are we being reminded of this, Monsignor Molthen?

Why dear saints?, all ye there, encrusted immaculately,

in stone cold tableaux, absorbed forever and today,

in emerald stained glass transfigurations, way up there,

high on the upper reaches of this long heavenly nave,

that stretches out like long arms wearing bracelets of infinity.

Why are we to be reminded of this?

The girls choir at St. Mary's still sing there.

Shh, be quiet as we step outside

through these green rectangular doors.

Shh! Listen...

We can still hear them up there,

in the translucent loft.

"...Well, there you be... on Hillview Court in 1923...That cake in your hands...Will it bleed if I cut it? Will it squeal when it is eaten by young teeth?... See the pasture of trees, distant beyond the back fence? It is there I will take you someday... after new seasons come and go, with their jackets unbuttoned, and shoes tossed aside... when we will both hear the music of surprised desire, simple and yet rhythmic..."

Don't Love Me Too Much

Don't love me too much.

It is a smothering pillow, please

I can barely breathe.

You won't let up

with your passionate touches,

your obsessed adulations on reverent knees,

your addled worship of every step I take

in your adoring presence; I must escape

your never-ending pining

for my next breath upon your nape;

Kindly keep your distance and do not touch,

for you are loving me too much!

Don't love me too much.

It is a paralyzing chain;

I cannot move here or there.

You will not refrain,

with your intense devotions,

your never-ending fawnings and motions,

with pipe, slippers and loveful extollings.

You refuse to at last pause

with your obvious obsequiousness, sitting there,

with manicured fingers swirling through my hair.

Kindly keep your distance and do not touch,

for you are loving me too much.

I Remember You

Yes, I remember you,

the dark-skinned girl,

dressed in tight corduroy,

unzipped on the floor there.

You were my lover that night in 1970;

We were wrestling

so smoothly, so passionately,

in the old brick house on Hoover street.

Remember honey? Just you and me

alone in the darkness,

kissing like kids crazy about each other,

listening to Hendrix on the oak console,

Electric Merman on axe in 1983,

Playing like a god from beneath

the fiery pinnacles of the Styx.

Remember? We were 18 and

wild with wordless desire.

I kissed you often that night

in the grey bluesy shadows,

embracing intensely

your perfumed, unbuttoned body,

on beige thick shag

by the open screen door,

with that benign breeze blowing in

softly and silently,

like the breath of whispering ghosts,

watching there, as we groped and licked,

two kneading felines, quivering,

insecure in the darkness,

our lips, slickered and lathered

in strawberry paste and love spit,

and our reaching tongues,

seared and slithering like caught tunas,

found electric connections

in the heaving nets

of aching fleshly onslaughts,

of mad touching embraces,

with esoteric teenage sweating

at silent midnight, in June,

when the jacarandas are in bloom.

Yes, I remember you,

The girl with the brown perfumed skin,

and those kissing smacking sucking lips

that spoke so loudly,

without ever saying a word.

"...he dropped dead thar, dead 'fore he hid the floor...in '41... as when he were born... he saw two spigots, two that gave, and two that took..."

Peeling Back the Bubble Wrap

Peeling back the bubble wrap on the ancient of days,

Back to when Nixon was still presiding,

He, leading with paranoid deliberations,

Sold his yeses to the Goldbricks, and the Mustard Men;

And while he was dipping into the rubbery tides of the latex surfers,

I found your shadowy pointing breasts, shivering outside my backdoor.

You were standing in the dark, waiting for me to turn the key…

1973 was the year you taught me how to love a woman;

You, at 21 years, and me, ensconced in the stereo-lit darkness,

Of my dimly-lit bedroom on Hoover street;

You, wearing a wool skirt and that ruffled low-curving blouse,

With those tan buttons, like a half dozen corks, ready to be popped,

And you, sitting at my black upright piano,

The 1907 Schumann, made of stubborn black mahogany, and

You, with your long curved nails, femininely tapping the ivories,

Soliciting an intimate song I have since forgotten, but can still hear,

Your cylindrical tan legs pressing the piano pedals,

Like a fragile dancer made of fine glass, and

You, exploring human desire with determined pressings.

And then, into your garlanded home we strolled,

Hand in hand; And with our lips, we cleared the stoney path

Leading into the sun garden, amongst the cats and the posies,

And found astonished silhouettes behind the peephole.

Still peeling back the bubble wrap on the ancient of days,

Back to when my door was locked, and a green candle burned therein;

I saw you in the naked flickering, riding the tree of silver ascensions,

And with five pulsing fingers, I eagerly picked your finest flowers, over there,

Inside the throbbing, sun-lit bed of this poised sun garden; then,

You told me you loved me. Told me what I never wanted to hear,

"Even now, with me on top of you, in this silent grinding darkness,

I cannot bring myself to lie and say, 'I love you.'

There is something about you I don't want to know.

Yours is a long and complicated book I do not wish to read.

Your mind I cannot calibrate, or truly understand, so…I am sorry.

I deserve to be called an ass, deserve to be brushed off like a gnat, but

With you, my shoes never seemed to fit. My ears never seemed to hear."

...when the copter went down, witnesses heard you scream...

"I am truly sorry."

...the old lady led the little boy into the musty kitchen and opened the third drawer. Inside were the taffy candies and the red lollipops. The little boy was silent as the talcum powder set in, and the black hard shoes moved forward. 1967 was the moment the little boy discovered the waning sunlight filtering through the distant window...

Such Innocent Madness

Listening to KHJ with the Real Don Steele,

playing it straight and loud on Boss Radio, with an

Elusive Butterfly wafting about, inside the tan '68 Caprice,

when his secret journey of a thousand eye blinks,

commenced painstakingly and torturously,

like a dead glacier on fire.

To the left there, by her brown-skinned sternum,

with her young heartbone cleaving through snail-paced deter-
minations,

he found her tender button throbbing,

beneath the cotton cover and the bleach,

there, in the excruciating darkness of teenage intensities;

You and he were reaching for the soul of an hour,

not stopping until constant time achieved the impossible stare
off,

between them and it,

between the air, and the touching;

between the voicing of electronic controllings,

and the perennial reaching for another red apple,

served au jus, with croutons, earwax and studied leanings.

Now, it is just another pause in the exertions of young exis-
tence,

another heaving mindmelt in the suburban fog,

where you and him once sat fifty years ago,

at the big oaken table beyond the archway there,

inside his mother's old musty house on Hoover street,

amidst the closed bedroom doors, the bougainvillea,

and the tacky green carpet with a dozen dog stains.

You sat there alluringly and decidedly silent,

with your long smooth legs opening and closing,

like a panting mouth, sucking in cigarette smoke in the dry
wind.

But it was such innocent madness,

what was done and said that distant night in 1969,

with you and him sitting decidedly close in the darkness,

within the secure, locked confines of the tan '68 Caprice.

Listen. Can you hear his bellowing voice through the speaker?

The Real Don Steele said it was April, when

all elusive butterflies swarm to the beat of the night,

the elusive time for young lovers to learn, and sigh.

IV. Scenes From the Sulcus

Poetic Collaborations by Stark Hunter and D. Lee

Poetry written 2017-2019

Time Is...

Time is the generous giver,

Which got me to thinking of the sea,

Through cosmic ebb and constraining flow,

I grabbed the knob and opened the door,

Opened the door to the remissive sonorous past,

Waves of effervescent ocean foam lapped at my knees,

My ten toes searched futilely-

The well-springs of ten thousand silent creatures;

Harboring my thoughts,

I laid out my strategy to proceed further,

Swim I must,

Through the rushing ripples

Of forgotten past days,

The abject poverty of loss,

A deterrent as it is, will not overcome,

Not overcome the close of stormy day;

The wind knows its dire destinations,

The frequency waves, soul searching,

Through black holes of lengthy duration,

Sought out my silent searching soul, sifting...

Sifting; future man bows his head.

In gratitude the salty waters washed,

Upon the shore, crusting, icing,

The delicate skin through time,

Through cosmic ebb, and constraining flow,

There, under the stars I waded,

Fell to my knees, like a stone,

As the grains of sand,

Swaddled my outline.

Sweet, Sweet Descendings

The meandering river slinks silently

In reluctant afterthought;

A flat stone shines in the sun's presence,

Gripped for flight, flies forward;

Water clouds dance in the rapids,

Celebrated with flames, and

The crying colors of terminations,

With the motion and swiftness of forethought,

Redacted and clothed in a mist;

As spiral complacencies nudge me from behind,

They seek to know my name.

They seek to harness the ghost prayers of a thousand decades,

As deities, in splendorous romancing,

With lips pursed for the joining of sparks,

Deliver the nudge and mouth the name,

All in sweet whispering buds,

As spreading flower petals lacerate the lacrimonious;

Falling, descending, down, down-

I see the green annihilations in the stars,

As the heavens, wet with anticipation,

In minds all enclosed in folds,

The whimpering few cry at twilight,

Trampling flowers and crusty coals.

Sweet sweet descendings,

Past the laughing ghosts of 1952,

They slice as a cleaver finds the core,

Divided, oh meandering slough,

The dance alights on an afterthought,

Redacted from behind, harnessed for years,

Sweet buds in green summer heat,

Petals and ghosts slice through,

The harrowing stars.

Lipstick Girls

1.   "When the Lipstick Girls Walk By"

You can push and shove your way,

Past all the driveling mindless mannequins,

Who bend over when the lipstick girls walk by.

No sense in being nice today or tomorrow,

Since every old fool is a phony anyway.

The Rhododendrons in my garden are emasculating the weeds,

And the acute disease of crotch rot has taken seed;

Maybe you think this is a sad joke,

Or an accidentally-thrown tomato of rotten thoughts?

Maybe you think my feelings have no skin?

Let's stop all the foolish talk now,

And let's hold hands. Let us seal the deal,

Here in this flesh garden,

This premeditated fling with skin cream and cancelled prayers.

Have you no decency?

Here is your hat, cover yourself.

2   "Of Meaningless Glances"

We, you and Me, can sit silently in a circle,

Inside this rigged invocation under the stars,

As the world of things, flung afar,

Rain down upon the solitude of which we strive.

Let us interlock, and enter into this dark dive,

This tavern of meaningless glances,

Of hopeful interludes in the dark;

I don't know what lurks in the closet, do you?

Shuttered away, though in close proximity to

An ambiguous opening that pulses eyelike;

There is no death in this dream dance;

The brass door knob is icy cold,

As the lipstick girls,

With lips of ice,

Turn the handle.

"Is there a hook for my stained hat?"

Let us sit, you and me, in this rigged circle,

The body of things are passionately torn away,

The tools of the trade reveal pulsingly,

Eroticism's charm, as tilted skirt,

And frozen glances askance, reveal

The mad scenes of the ghost dancers,

As doors, mysterious to the crowds, close

And are locked;

The icy shade of winter's hem is

Bathed in luminous light,

The darkness washes onto the drains,

Down to the ocean's mouth.

3   "An Archway!"

an archway opens on to a soporific plaza,

that pours outwardly in colorful asymmetric

displays, that once incited the bones of an organic past

steeped in a rich broth, an ancestral heaving stew

quietly simmering to a point of boil.

the humble ones, once alive to the core, move to and fro,

cornered and stultified by conventions, babbling broken man-
tras,

they attempt to sooth the spirits daunting deadly pricks

the lipstick girls of the labial folds, that exist beyond the pale

of a refracting sun's light, hover between ghostly spheres

of a lost sacerdotal history, wet with gloss,

yearningly enchant youthful acolytes who, painted in salacious

priestly pastels, patterned up to placate the Ones,

fully endowed and exuding in virginal carnality,

fall willingly into their own demise, caressed by the

spreading tongs, in the act of sacrifice.

An archway opens out to a thriving, heaving plaza.

We Are The Stardust Men

Dedicated to T.S. Eliot

We are the stardust men,

the wayward stardust catching men,

dalliances of mind and shadow occur openly,

As we have cast off our anchors

And await the tidal sway,

The open expanse of deep landscape,

Beckons the siren call.

We are the seeing men, the blind

far-sighted beauty-seeking tin men;

repercussions of old laws and rituals,

like drowning petrels, hundreds of them,

dot the landscape.

Where, oh where in the excrement of human habitation,

the many-layered strata of ham-fisted movements

did we fall out of our fantasies,

like stones from the shallow well.

We are the stardust men, looking for an atomic biscuit.

We are the rocky and mortar men,

Made of skin and water and fear;

Ham-fisted soul searchers, dressed in layered strata,

The stardust men,

Wrapped in haze and cloud,

As smoke wafting upward, streaming outward,

Unlike the tides clockwork geared up and locked in,

the conditioned we, breaking free,

Leaping out of the trees;

We are the blue-sky looking men,

the running free, cloud-seeking breathing men,

out to find brazen perfumes in the stunted dooryard,

out to seek other floral arrangements in the embrace.

We are the stardust catchers,

The brazen thumb tappers upon lost trellises,

All nets and hooks, attempting to catch

an elusive ambiguity.

The Glistening of Formica Memories

Stepping on wet lateral stones,

at the Source of the Bicuspid,

three timeless tree-girls,

dressed in Colorado feathers,

urged on to fly,

as far as the harbinger's voice,

reverberating from the source

and onward to eternity's margins,

assume the mad ascendancies

to the highest peak, the farthest city;

their three steeped voices slicing

the formica memories

into shards with bitter fingers.

The glistening call,

of that farthest city,

wallows in the mirage

of seeming imaginations,

of fluid want with foreshadowing

remnants of lateral intricacies,

of standard practices

in the unseen interludes;

why is it when the wind blows

from the source we can listen,

but not hear?

Has memory succumbed

to the vacuum of time and warp?

On which wetted lateral stones

does source-wind lay out

the patterned template?

But now the feathers amerce

the wind's seasoned harbingers,

plying the stars to find their elàn

amidst the mirages,

urged on to fly, ascending lofty peaks,

beckoned by eternity's margins,

three arbored fems,

imagination becoming flesh,

stars and stones merging,

as timeless as formica;

their fleshly lateral stones

finding the Source of the Bicuspid.

About The Author

Born in Whittier, California in 1952, Stark Hunter was an English teacher for 38 years before retiring from the classroom in 2017. He has also written and published 8 books, which are available on Amazon.com and Barnes & Noble.com: In A Gadda Da Vida, published in 2002, Carnivorous Avenues, a poetry volume published in 2004, Flies, a short novel published in 2005, Private Diaries, a satire published in 2006, Voices From Clark Cemetery, a poetry volume published in 2013, Cocktails For the Soul, a poetry anthology published in 2013, Voices From Mt. Olive Cemetery, a poetry volume published in 2018, and Digested by the Dust, another poetry anthology, published in 2018.

Mr. Hunter is also a published photographer, having one of his photographs included in the book, Photography Vibes, Best of Edition in 2008.

Fourteen of Mr. Hunter's poems from Voices From Clark Cemetery were adopted and set to music by Dr. George Mabry, composer and former conductor of the Nashville Symphony Chorus, for his work, Voices, a musical drama which was performed at Austin Peay State University in Clarksville, Tennessee in 2015.

Mr. Hunter's poetry works can be perused at Poetrysoup.com, and his photography is on display at JPGMag. Com. Mr. Hunter's blog site is Stark Hunter's Mind Tavern@wordpress.com., and his website is www.starkhunter.com.

Mr. Hunter is married with two daughters, a granddaughter, and resides in Chino Hills, California.

www.ingramcontent.com/pod-product-compliance
Lightning Source LLC
Chambersburg PA
CBHW032033040426
42449CB00007B/880